The Rainforest Book

HOW YOU CAN SAVE THE WORLD'S RAINFORESTS

Scott Lewis

with the Natural Resources Defense Council

Edited by Dwight Holing

Los Angeles

This book is dedicated
to all those who care about the fate of the Earth,
and to those committed to saving her

Published in the United States by Living Planet Press, 558 Rose Avenue, Venice, California 90291

Distributed by Publishers Group West, Emeryville, California

Interior design and page layout: Madeleine Budnick
Cover design: Sharon Smith
Additional cover design and hand lettering: William Whitehead
Cover and interior illustrations: Mercedes McDonald
Word processing: Hazel Westney
Copyediting: Carol Henderson
Production coordination: Zipporah Collins
Printing and binding: R. R. Donnelley and Sons

To order this book, please see page 112—or look in your local bookstore. Discounts are available for bulk orders.

 Printed on 100% recycled Crosspoint Sycamore paper

Manufactured in the United States of America
Library of Congress catalog card number 90-70819

Contents

Never doubt that a small group of thoughtful, committed citizens can change the world. Indeed, it's the only thing that ever has.

— *Margaret Mead*

Acknowledgments

Staff members of the Natural Resources Defense Council who provided an invaluable contribution to this effort include Eric Washburn, Glenn Prickett, Jacob Scherr, Robert F. Kennedy, Jr., Faith Campbell, Chuck Clusen, Suzzette Delgado-Mendoza, Laura King, Linda Lopez, Susan Miller, and David Wirth. My thanks to them all.

My grateful appreciation to the following people whose generous contributions of time, effort, resources, and advice made the writing of this book possible: Randy Hayes and the Rainforest Action Network, Linda Neale at Friends of the Earth/U.K., Luke Cole and Jeffrey Avina of the Vincent J. Skinsky Foundation, Martha Cappelletti of the Smithsonian Institution Traveling Exhibition Service, Frank Almeda and Brian Lym at the California Academy of Sciences, and Laurence Lewis.

For their professionalism, commitment, and enthusiasm, I thank Stephen Tukel and Joshua Horwitz, my publishers, and Dwight Holing, my editor.

Finally, for their soul-support, my sincere appreciation to Thomas Valtin, Tania and Laura Rose, my parents, Carol and Kenneth Lewis, and my sister, Kathleen Lewis.

Preface

Three hundred million years ago, the land to the east of my home in Utah was not desert but jungle, similar to the Amazon Basin. Strange creatures dwelt in a tropical world marked by towering trees, gigantic ferns, and flowering vines. Since that time, glaciers have come and gone, the weather has changed, and the rainforests in these parts have disappeared. The only trace of the plants and animals that once lived here is frozen in fossilized rocks and muds scattered about the desert floor.

Today, another change is taking place that is causing rainforests to disappear. Only this time the cause is not as natural. Every day thousands of acres of tropical forests fall, victims of chain saws, burning, and shortsighted government policies. In what amounts to a geological blink of the eye, we are witnessing the extinction of more species of plants and animals than all those that disappeared in the amount of time it took evolution to kill off the dinosaurs.

Global warming, biological extinction, annihilation of native peoples—these are just a few of the costs associated with tropical deforestation.

Although the assault on Earth's rainforests is indeed critical, there is room for hope. Already, worldwide attention is being focused on the problem. And even more reassuring is the fact that there are things all of us can do to help save the rainforests.

The Rainforest Book comes at exactly the right moment. Its emphasis on practical solutions makes it an invaluable guide to help us reform the policies of the past that have fostered such widespread destruction. It was written with the Natural Resources Defense Council, a national organization that has a solid record of research and advocacy on behalf of the environment.

The book explains why the rainforests are important not only to wildlife but also to the well-being of all of us, no matter where we live. While it points out in no uncertain terms that humankind is the cause of the problem, it shows that we are the solution as well—that is, if we choose to act.

— Robert Redford
Sundance, Utah
1990

INTRODUCTION

Tropic of Concern

Tropic of Concern

Place your palm lightly upon the fattest part of a spinning globe and the world's tropics will pass beneath your hand. Within this enormous midsection of the Earth live more species of plants and animals than in the rest of the planet combined. The tropics support an astonishing array of lush, dense, and fertile rainforests—the product of drenching rain and brilliant sunshine. Colorful and unique native flora and fauna make them veritable Edens, but these gardens are as fragile as dreams. Rainforests and their dependent inhabitants are extremely vulnerable to human disturbance. The rate of their destruction staggers the mind and sickens the soul. In the second it takes that globe spinning beneath your fingers to make a single rotation, an entire acre of rainforest will have disappeared. Forever.

The abundance of life in the rainforest is matched by its diversity. More species of plants grow in the tropical forests of Panama than in all of Europe. In a Peruvian wildlife reserve that covers half the land area of the city of San Francisco live 545 species of birds, 100 kinds of dragonflies, and 792 types of butterflies. Twenty to 50 percent of the plants there have yet to be named. Nearly 1,500 species of birds—that's 16 percent of all the species of birds in the world—nest in the rainforests of Indonesia. Nearly one-quarter of those are endemic, meaning they occur naturally nowhere else in the world.

Tropical forests contain a bounty of riches, from hardwoods to food products to vital medications for heart disease and cancer. Pharmacologists have identified 3,000 plants as having cancer-fighting properties; 70 percent of them grow in the rainforest. The rosy periwinkle produces a substance used to combat childhood leukemia. Diosgenin, which is made from rainforest plants in Guatemala, Mexico, and Belize, is the active ingredient in cortisone.

Tropical plants also have industrial uses. Next time you touch down safely in an airplane, thank a rubber tree. The tires were most likely made from rubber tapped from a tree growing in a rainforest. In Brazil, the copaiba tree produces a sap that is used to fuel diesel engines.

Rainforests also play an essential role in our weather. Forested areas absorb solar energy, helping to drive the circulation of the atmosphere. This phenomenon affects wind and rainfall patterns worldwide. Tropical vegetation also contains enormous quantities of carbon, which clearing releases as carbon dioxide. Protecting tropical forests thus helps prevent global warming —a phenomenon commonly called the "greenhouse effect." Rainforests reduce erosion and provide natural buffers against wind damage and flooding along coastal areas. When a storm blows in from sea, the trees growing near shore soften its punch.

Tropical rainforests are a rich and animated celebration of the diversity and wonder of life. Unfortunately, celebration is quickly turning into tragedy. Around the world, rainforests are being destroyed at an alarming rate. In Papua New Guinea, vast areas of the primeval jungle are being uprooted as miners plunder the island for copper and gold. The Amazon is being slashed and burned to make way for cattle and farms. The roar of chain saws drowns the songs of birds in Southeast Asia as loggers cut an ever-widening swath through the wilderness. Closer to home, resort and energy development is shrinking the rainforests of Hawai`i (native spelling) and the Virgin Islands, while industry and urban sprawl threaten Puerto Rico's national and commonwealth forests.

Already, half the Earth's tropical forests have been burned, bulldozed, and obliterated. The rest are being wiped out at the shocking rate of 35.2 million acres a year. That's 67 acres a minute—a football field a second. Each year an area the size of New York State vanishes forever. If this pace continues, most of the rainforests will be gone before the end of the century.

As the forests are destroyed, so are the myriad species that depend on them for survival. Recent studies estimate that tropical deforestation wipes out 17,000 species of plants and animals per year—species that exist nowhere else. That's about 48 species made extinct every day, or 2 an hour.

Wildlife species aren't the only living creatures at risk of extinction from deforestation. People live in the rainforests, too. Throughout the rainforests of Asia, Latin America, and Africa, indigenous tribal groups—native people—maintain traditional cultures, as they have for thousands of years. The loss of the rainforest threatens their physical and cultural survival.

Finally, tropical deforestation may spell doom for all of us. All species of life on the planet are bound by a complex network of interdependencies. Each time a species is removed, the foundation of life grows weaker. Who knows how many species can be lost before the global ecosystem collapses? More immediately, how many more trees in the rainforests can we afford to lose before global warming becomes irreversible, causing widespread drought, rising seas, and other disastrous environmental changes?

The causes of tropical deforestation are complex. Agriculture, logging, and ranching all result in the clearing or degradation of thousands of square miles annually. However, to reduce

the level of deforestation, we must address the underlying causes, such as population growth, poverty, foreign debt, and multilateral aid policies.

Although the fate of the rainforest is indeed dire, there are reasons to be hopeful. In recent years, international awareness of the catastrophe of rainforest destruction has reached new heights, and public concern and involvement are growing. Many tropical countries—Brazil, Indonesia, Thailand, and the Philippines, for instance—have taken the first steps to protect their rainforests. More must be done, however. Much, much more.

That's where you come in. All of us can help save the rainforests. We can begin right here at home. Our own domestic tropical forests need protection. We can bring public pressure to bear to make sure the government acts to save them. By preserving our own tropical forests, we can demonstrate our environmental commitment to humankind. We must not underestimate the impact our own natural-resource management policies can have on developing countries. The preservation of our ecologically unique and biologically diverse old-growth forests in Washington, Oregon, and Alaska, as well as of our tropical forests in Hawai`i, Puerto Rico, the Virgin Islands, and American Samoa, can illustrate the importance of long-term ecological values over short-term economic gain.

At the same time, we can influence foreign governments to increase their protection efforts as well. For example, the United States can work to alter the policies of multilateral banks, such as the World Bank, to ensure that funded projects are ecologically sustainable. Where appropriate, we can and must exert economic pressure as consumers. Certain products on the market hasten the destruction of tropical forests. Not buying them can send an important signal to nations that don't manage their tropical natural resources wisely, and to corporations that profit from forests' destruction.

As individuals, too, we can set an example. By recycling, carpooling, and conserving water and energy, we can provide a model for developing countries to evaluate the impact of their own environmental policies.

The causes of tropical deforestation are complex but not incomprehensible. This book will help you understand why rainforests are important and what you can do to protect them. It provides an introduction to the characteristics of tropical forests and to the primary causes and consequences of tropical forest destruction.

The causes of tropical forest loss vary from country to country, and generalizations are difficult to make. But this does not preclude us from taking action to prevent deforestation through our governmental policies and through our own lifestyles. In Chapter 5, you'll find a guide to the things you can do in your own life to help save the rainforests. Chapter 6 contains a directory of organizations and literature that can supply you with additional information about rainforests.

The fate of the world's tropical forests rests with each and every one of us. By becoming informed, by becoming involved, you can help ensure the survival of hundreds of species and, along with them, our own.

CHAPTER ONE

Under the Canopy

Under the Canopy

What tropical rainforests are like

Dawn in the upper Amazon Basin. A symphony of life resumes its familiar refrain as it has each day for millions of years. Flocks of orange and green parrots glide over an emerald sea of treetops. A colony of aggressive red howler monkeys scrambles through the branches in search of fruit. On the ground a giant anteater snakes its velvety, trunk-like snout under a fallen limb as termites scurry for cover. Shiny orchid bees shake off the torpor of night and begin their busy commute among the white, magenta, and crimson blossoms that slowly unfurl to meet the fierce morning sun. As dawn gives way to day, life assumes its rich eternal rhythm in an ancient dance of birth, hunger, growth, death, and decay.

Good morning and welcome to the most alive place on Earth, the tropical rainforest. Part of a 3.4 million-square-mile green band that encircles the equator, rainforests are home to over half of all living things—this in an area that covers less than 7 percent of the land surface of the globe. In addition to the vast Amazon rainforest, tropical rainforests flourish in Africa, Asia,

Central America, and here in the United States—in Hawai`i, Puerto Rico, American Samoa, and the U.S. Virgin Islands.

Our earliest images of a rainforest came from Hollywood. Scores of grade B jungle movies, complete with a Great White Hunter hacking his way through a seemingly impenetrable wall of vines, conspired to convince us that all rainforests were dark, forbidding places filled with murderous natives, cunning man-eating animals, and poisonous plants. The truth is more complex.

To begin with, there is no one kind of tropical rainforest. The term is just a handy way of referring to a variety of different habitats that occur on either side of the equator between the Tropics of Cancer and Capricorn. Scientists divide these places into three broad categories: tropical dry forests, tropical moist forests, and true tropical rainforests. Each is further divided into subcategories based on such factors as elevation, soil type, and climatic conditions.

Most tropical rainforests fall into the "true" category. You'll find them closest to the equator at low elevations. They are wetter and warmer than the other two types, and are drenched by 160 to 400 inches of rain per year. New York City, by comparison, averages 43 inches annually, San Francisco about 20 inches a year. Rainforest temperatures average 80 degrees Fahrenheit year-round. These conditions have made tropical forests the most diversely populated places on Earth in terms of plant and animal life.

Layers of life

Tropical rainforest vegetation grows in distinct layers, each forming a unique habitat for dependent plants and animals. The top layer of the rainforest consists of emergent trees that tower 160 feet or higher and poke randomly out of the dense canopy directly below.

Sneaky snakes

Some rainforest plants and animals mimic each other's appearance in order to hide from predators or sneak up on prey. Snakes look like vines, moths like hummingbirds, and butterflies like leaves.

The canopy is the forest's most luxuriant layer. A dense mass of treetops, vines, and other plants, it rises some 100 to 130 feet above the forest floor. Most rainforest life grows or dwells in the canopy. Although from the ground the canopy appears as a solid green mass, it is actually a mad profusion of color. Flowers bloom in a brilliant spectrum of hues and shades—there are bright yellows, every shade of green, flaming reds, and regal purples. Orchids blush from pink to scarlet, bromeliads range from snowy white to chocolate.

Beneath the emergent trees and canopy spreads the understory, a tangle of seedlings, saplings, bushes, and shrubs that grow as high as 50 to 80 feet above the ground. The bottom layer is the forest floor. Plant growth here is limited because the thick blanket of vegetation formed by the overhanging canopy blocks all but 1 to 2 percent of the available sunlight. Aside from a scattering of leaves and decaying plant matter, seedlings, and small plants, the floor of a tropical rainforest is typically bare.

The great green tapestry

While the richest temperate forests of the United States contain at most 25 species of trees, a single acre of tropical rainforest supports 60 to 80 tree species. Studies of the rainforests of Borneo, for example, have identified 2,500 tree species in an area half the size of Great Britain. By contrast, Great Britain claims only 35 native species of tree. All of North America boasts only 865 native tree species.

You'll find plenty of plants in the rainforests as well. Of the 12,000 species of ferns identified worldwide, 11,000 are tropical; three-quarters of the world's mosses are tropical as well. Rainforests also contain an astonishing array of climbing plants and vines. Some can grow as thick as your body and reach hundreds of feet in length. These creepers depend on host plants and trees for physical support. As long as they grow along the forest floor or in the understory, their leaves remain relatively small, helping them conserve vital energy. But once the leaves reach the bright sunlight of the canopy, they grow huge to acquire energy. Some can reach six feet in length!

Many tropical plants grow on other plants. Epiphytes (literally meaning "air plants") sprout on trees. Usually their roots

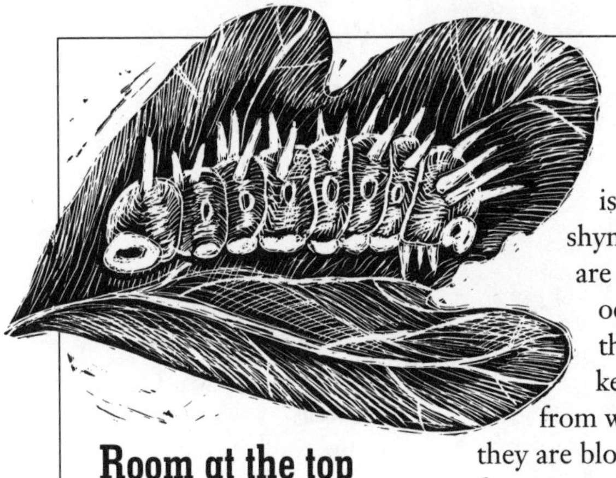

Room at the top

The trees in rainforest canopies are rarely interlocking; their crowns typically stand about three feet from each other. This is known as crown shyness, and scientists are not sure why it occurs. Popular theories include keeping trees safe from wind damage as they are blown about in the frequent tropical storms, or preventing tree-eating caterpillars from getting from tree to tree.

don't even reach the ground. They derive all their water and nourishment either directly from the air or from material that is caught in the nooks and crannies of trees far above the forest floor. Approximately 28,000 species of epiphytes have been identified worldwide. The best known are orchids. Close to 50 species of orchid have been found blooming on a single rainforest tree.

The bromeliads, cousins of the pineapple, are another type of epiphyte. Bromeliad leaves are arranged in the shape of a pitcher in order to trap rainwater and debris falling from the canopy above. As the debris decomposes, it forms a kind of soil that supports still other types of plants. Some bromeliads form symbiotic relationships with their hosts. Some trees grow tiny roots out of their uppermost branches and tap into the nutrients trapped by their flowering tenants. Water pooled inside a bromeliad can also become a home to frogs, salamanders, crabs, and aquatic plants and insects. Sometimes these "bucket plants"

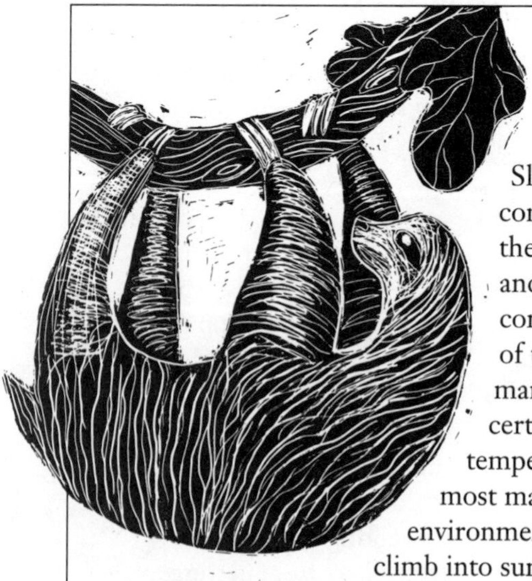

Warning: sloth overhead

Sloths, one of the most common large mammals in the rainforests of Central and South America, can constitute up to two-thirds of the weight of all living mammals, or biomass, in certain areas. A sloth's body temperature, unlike that of most mammals, varies with the environment. Consequently, sloths climb into sunny openings among the branches and hang there for hours to absorb solar heat.

REDISCOVERED PRIMATE

The Hairy-eared Dwarf Lemur

We are primates. So are monkeys and apes. In the soggy rainforests on the island of Madagascar, off the coast of Africa, lives the world's tiniest known primate, the hairy-eared dwarf lemur.

The dwarf lemur is five inches long, not counting its furry seven-inch tail. Shaped like a little brown mouse, it weighs just three and a half ounces.

Scientists had thought the tiny primate extinct, but recently a West German biologist, Bernhard Meier, ventured into the heart of Madagascar's last remaining rainforest and caught sight of the elusive creature. This find was important for two reasons: First, the hairy-eared dwarf lemur is the only surviving species of a whole genus of lemurs. Second, its rediscovery signals just how little we know about rainforests and how much remains to be discovered.

grow so heavy after a rainstorm that they break the branch they're growing on or even pull down the entire tree.

Unlike the temperate forests of North America, which have fewer tree species per acre but more of each species, the rainforest has lots of tree species per acre but only a few of each. This limited population of individuals in a given area makes the species more vulnerable. Clear even a small part of the forest and many species could become extinct. When the trees go, so do the species that depend on them—everything from insects to birds to mammals.

All creatures rare and wonderful

The stunning profusion of rainforest tree and plant species supports an equally diverse number of animals. Take the rainforests of Southeast Asia, for example. They support an estimated 656 mammal species and 850 amphibian species—almost one-third of all those in the world. By comparison, Europe contains only 134 native mammal species.

Each layer of rainforest, from the forest floor to the emergent trees, is a unique habitat; animals from one level rarely venture into other levels. The canopy, the level richest in plant life, is also home to more animals than any other part of the forest. In one study of a rainforest, half the mammals (not including bats) were found to live in trees. In temperate forests only about 15 percent of mammals are considered arboreal.

Mammals are the largest animals in the rainforest. Ground-level species include elephant, deer, tapir, wild pig, various species of cat, and, in the forests of Southeast Asia, even rhinoceros, though they are extremely rare. Tree-dwelling mammals include such primates as gibbon, howler monkey, spider monkey, and chimpanzee. The gorilla lives in the African rainforest, while the loris and tarsier, nocturnal cousins of the monkey, make their home in the trees of Southeast Asia. The orangutan depends on the rainforests of Borneo and Sumatra for survival. It is one of the world's largest primates; males can weigh over 200 pounds. The largest South American monkey is the rare pale-orange muriqui of Brazil, also known as the woolly spider monkey. Only a few hundred muriquis remain in the wild. Other tree dwellers include various types of sloths, marsupials, squirrels, rats, and mice.

Tropical forests support a variety of felines, including tiger, ocelot, leopard, and jaguar. The fossa, Madagascar's largest carnivore, is a large, reddish-brown cat that preys on tree-dwelling lemurs and other small mammals and birds. Widespread destruction of its home has left it in danger of extinction. Many of the rainforest's other beautiful feline predators are also endangered as a result of habitat destruction and the fur trade.

The most eye-catching rainforest inhabitants are feathered. Splashed with bold, beautiful markings, birds such as toucan,

Big bird

The cassowary, a huge, flightless bird native to New Guinea, stands nearly as tall as a man and can run through the rainforest with great speed. A ferocious bird, it has legs strong enough to rip open a human belly with one swipe.

macaw, bird of paradise, hornbill, and flycatcher provide a dazzling display of color against the great green backdrop of the forest. The number of bird species is astonishing. One out of three bird species found in the world nests in the rainforest—some 2,600 species in all. One wildlife reserve in Costa Rica has more bird species than the entire North American continent.

Color isn't the only characteristic that distinguishes rainforest birds. The harpy eagle is the largest and most powerful eagle in the world. Males can weigh over 20 pounds and stand three feet tall. Their prey consists of deer, sloth, monkey, opossum, tree porcupine, and anteater. Though their territory extends from southern Mexico to northern Argentina, these magnificent predators are extremely rare. Another rainforest raptor is the laughing falcon, so named for its cry, which has been compared to the laugh of a human being driven mad. This aerial speedster plucks snakes slinking along the rainforest's upper branches and eats them for its supper.

The rainforest boasts many different species of snake.The fer-de-lance is the most dangerous. Its venom can kill within seconds.The largest python in the world also hails from the rainforest; an Indonesian species stretches the tape at over 30 feet. Although they have been known to eat the occasional human, these scaly giants prefer to dine on monkey, bird, and pig.

Of all the rainforest residents, insects are the most numerous. Estimates of the number of different species reach up to 80 million. Over 240 species of army ants alone have been identified. Biologists have counted nearly 300 different kinds of butterflies in a square mile of the African rainforest. A national park in Sarawak, a province of Malaysia, supports 3,000 species of butterfly and moth in a dramatic range of color and size. Imagine a butterfly with a 12-inch wingspan!

What makes rainforests so valuable and so biologically intriguing is not what we know about them, but what we don't. Who knows how many species of plants and animals remain to be discovered?

CHAPTER TWO

Forests of Plenty

Forests of Plenty

Why we should preserve rainforests

Tropical rainforests are nature's celebration of life. In them you will find more kinds of plants and animals than in any other place you can go on Earth. As the forests vanish, part of life's richness is slowly lost, acre by acre, day by day. With this loss of plant and animal species, many benefits to humankind also vanish, for rainforests are a treasure house of foods, medicines, and other resources we have only begun to discover. Fewer than 1 percent of tropical forest species have even been studied for their potential usefulness.

Rainforests are home to millions of indigenous people who can share with us the forests' secrets. The forests also regulate the world's weather, and their protection will help prevent the global warming known as the greenhouse effect. Finally, the very abundance of life that makes rainforests so unique is a resource itself. The gene pool of the rainforest—its biological diversity—is the foundation on which all life on the planet, including our own, depends for survival.

People of the forest

Tropical forests around the world provide a home for an estimated 140 million people, many of them indigenous tribal people. An estimated 700 distinct tribal groups live in Papua New Guinea, approximately 200 tribes live in the Congo Basin of Africa, and at least 60 groups remain in Colombia. Overall, more than 1,000 indigenous tribal groups still survive worldwide. Many maintain ancient forms of human culture. The Penan of Malaysia and the Efe of Zaire, for instance, still rely on hunting and gathering for survival.

Although Western culture has a long tradition of destroying such societies, we can no longer tolerate such chauvinism. These people deserve to live as they always have, just as much as we deserve to live our own life-style. In fact, their cultures should command our respect by virtue of the fact that they are sustainable, something our "educated" Western culture has yet to attain.

Furthermore, we can learn much from the accumulated customs, traditions, and folklore of these people. They are an irreplaceable resource. They can teach us about medicinal and edible plants, farming and irrigation methods, and ways to protect crops from disease and insects. The Lua tribe in northern Thailand, for instance, grows 75 food crops and 21 different medicinal plants. The Hanunoo people in the Philippines have developed 430 rainforest crops. The Lacandon Maya in southeastern Mexico use complex irrigation schemes and sophisticated agricultural systems that utilize intercropping and agroforestry techniques. These techniques allow them to survive in the rainforest without depleting its natural resources. Corn, potatoes, tomatoes, peanuts, avocados, cashews, and vanilla are among the foods we have learned about from the Indians of Latin America and other early forest communities. Indigenous

VANISHING CULTURES

The Penan and Kayan People

The Penan and Kayan tribespeople practice hunting and gathering and small-scale agriculture in the Malaysian province of Sarawak, much as their ancestors did for nearly 50,000 years. Ten years ago Malaysian logging companies began moving onto the island and have cleared over one-third of its forests already. Loggers cut down close to five square miles of forest a day, and food shortages, flooding, and droughts are spreading across the island.

The logging has also caused widespread siltation and pollution of rivers and streams throughout Sarawak, making fishing impossible and thus depriving the Penan and Kayan of an important food supply. With no hope of continuing their traditional life-style in the areas devastated by logging, half the remaining Penan now live in hastily built shacks and suffer disease and malnutrition previously unknown on the island.

Beginning in the spring of 1987, the Penan and Kayan people began to blockade the logging roads into their rainforest homelands to protect their traditional way of life. The government responded by arresting hundreds of tribespeople. The logging continues.

rainforest dwellers also gave us quinine, the cure for malaria, along with a host of other medicinal substances.

Unfortunately, indigenous tribal people are facing increasing pressure as the impact of the "modern world" spreads to the most remote reaches of the rainforests. No tribal community is free from the risk of destruction, either by annihilation or by assimilation. Since Western civilization "discovered" the Amazon Basin, for example, the population of indigenous Indians there has plummeted from an estimated 6 to 9 million people to fewer than 200,000. In the last century, 87 unique tribes have been exterminated in Brazil alone.

We are all enriched by the diverse and unique cultures that populate the world. These different cultures make up the global tapestry of human society. Every time a culture, no matter how small or remote, is lost, we all become a little poorer.

Mangoes, manioc, and more

When you drink a cup of coffee, peel a banana, or sprinkle a little cinnamon on your toast, do you ever think about where these foods came from? The answer is a tropical forest. These and a thousand other products we've come to depend on are all derived from plants and trees that grow in the tropics. The range of rainforest products stretches from the latex in your house paint to the tires on your car to the rubber ball your kids play catch with to such life-saving medicines as anesthetics, cancer drugs, and antibiotics.

Tropical forests are a veritable cornucopia. Rice, coffee, tea, chocolate, lemons, oranges, bananas, and pineapples are among the dozens of tropical foods that have found their way into domestic cuisine. Many of the agricultural crops we consider domestic actually originated in the tropics. In fact, only 2 percent of crop production in the United States is based on native species. Species that have not been marketed yet could add even more variety to our food selection. So far, only 15 of an estimated 2,500 edible fruit species from tropical forests are considered commercially important.

Derivatives from tropical plants are also making important contributions to the food marketplace. For example, in Japan and Europe, thaumatin, a nonfattening sweetener developed from tropical plants, was recently introduced. It is 1,600 times sweeter than sucrose. It may soon be seen on U.S. shelves.

Species and varieties brought in from tropical forests have not only added to the diversity of our diet, they have also improved the crop strains we currently enjoy. Tropical plants can enhance the quality of domestic crops through hybridization. As a result of crossbreeding tropical strains with domestic varieties, world coffee and sugar cane crops have been saved from devastation by disease. A wild cousin of domestic corn interbred with domestic varieties may result in a disease-resistant strain that won't need to be replanted every year, as current varieties do.

Natural bugbusters

Insect damage to crops in the United States alone costs $2 billion per year, and up to half of the insect pests in this country have grown resistant to inorganic pesticides. In recent years there has been a growing trend toward using natural pest controls. Pesticide-resistant insects are just one of the reasons for this change. Another has to do with concerns over the health and environmental risks posed by chemical-based pesticides.

The search for natural pest control has turned to tropical forests. Many tropical plants have developed natural defenses against insect attacks, defenses that include substances that can be used as natural insecticides for domestic crops. In addition, certain tropical insects are being tested for use as "counter-pests," natural enemies used to combat troubling native insect populations. Reliance on these natural bugbusters appears to

Fowl play

All domestic chickens are descendants of four species of Asian jungle fowl.

make economic sense. According to the U.S. Department of Agriculture, importing counterpests brings about $30 of benefit for every dollar invested.

For health's sake

The tropical forest is a fantastic medicine cabinet. Many tropical plants contain natural ingredients that can be turned into antibiotics, painkillers, heart drugs, and hormones. One-fourth of all prescription drugs sold in the United States contain plant-derived compounds. The estimated worldwide value of these prescription drugs was $51 billion in 1989. Approximately 5 percent of all plant species are believed to have medicinal properties, yet of the thousands of tropical plants, fewer than 1 percent have been studied for their possible uses.

The U.S. National Cancer Institute has identified 3,000 plants as having anticancer properties; of these, 70 percent hail from the rainforest. The rosy periwinkle, to name one, produces a substance used to counteract leukemia in children. Thanks to this tropical plant, a child with lymphocytic leukemia now has a 99 percent chance of remission, compared to 20 percent before the drug was discovered. The substance is also being used to fight Hodgkin's disease, breast cancer, and cervical cancer.

Diosgenin, the active ingredient in birth control pills and cortisone—a drug used to treat rashes, infections, and skin irritation—is a steroid originally derived from plants found in the rainforests of Mexico and Guatemala. Quinine, derived from the bark of the tropical cinchona tree, was the first substance determined to be effective against malaria, a disease that was once responsible for the death of millions worldwide. Synthetic antimalaria drugs have been modeled after this natural disease-fighter, but in recent years such drugs have been found to be losing their effectiveness against certain malaria strains that have grown resistant. This is not the case with drugs still derived from the natural extracts of cinchona bark, which

Zombie frogs

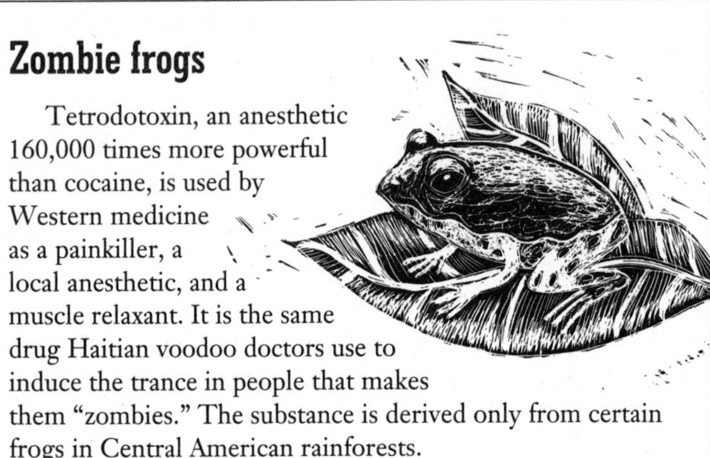

Tetrodotoxin, an anesthetic 160,000 times more powerful than cocaine, is used by Western medicine as a painkiller, a local anesthetic, and a muscle relaxant. It is the same drug Haitian voodoo doctors use to induce the trance in people that makes them "zombies." The substance is derived only from certain frogs in Central American rainforests.

hasn't lost any of its effectiveness despite more than a century of use.

Tree power

Rainforest substances are used in everything from cosmetics to automobile tires. Bus and car tires are often up to 40 percent natural rubber, which has better elasticity and heat resistance than synthetic rubber. Airplane and bulldozer tires are often made almost entirely out of natural rubber. This translates into an economic bonanza for rubber-exporting countries. Natural rubber exports are worth over $3 billion per year and have become the fourth largest agricultural export from the Third World. Rubber can be tapped without cutting down trees. It is a renewable resource.

Rubber trees grown on plantations in Malaysia and other countries in Southeast Asia have become the primary sources of natural rubber. But native species in Brazil are still needed for crossbreeding with the plantation varieties to give them more effective disease resistance and tolerance to cold and drought.

Other wild varieties yield different kinds of latex which improve rubber mixtures.

Shelter from the storm

Tropical forests perform a variety of environmental functions. They can prevent and alleviate floods and droughts, retain topsoil, and buffer the impact of storms.

Rainforests cover less than 7 percent of the Earth's surface, yet they receive almost half of all the rain that falls on land. Forests absorb rainfall and slowly release it into rivers and streams. When rainforests are intact, rivers run full and clear throughout the year. But when the forests are cut, rivers swell with muddy sediment after rains and shrink during dry spells. Flooding and droughts prevail, and soil erosion accelerates.

The effect can be devastating. For example, in 1988 a storm in Thailand caused widespread flooding and destruction. Some 400 people were killed, and 250,000 were left homeless. Property damage exceeded $5 million. The destructive nature of the storm was made worse by extensive tropical deforestation. Similar problems are found in tropical forests throughout the world. The clearing of one-third of the rainforest in the province of Sarawak in Malaysia has led to widespread flooding, droughts, and food shortages. Recent droughts in Africa and devastating mud slides in Brazil are also the result of deforestation. Worldwide, approximately 1 billion people are periodically disrupted by flooding and soil and water degradation caused by tropical deforestation.

The erosion that results from deforestation also causes massive amounts of silt to wash downstream. Siltation clogs dams and canals, which causes river beds to rise and increases flooding. The impact can be costly. In Panama, for example, siltation caused by runoff from deforested areas and dams on rivers that feed into the canal has blocked the canal on occasion, forcing ships to sail all the way around the tip of South America.

In Asia, Africa, and South America, siltation has reduced the effective life of some dams by as much as 50 percent.

Tropical forests also provide a natural defense against hurricanes, cyclones, and typhoons. Eighty to 100 tropical storms form around the world every year. When these storms move over land, tropical forests absorb the punch of howling winds and, in coastal areas, prevent storm-lashed tides from eroding beaches and shorelines. As development eliminates tropical forest areas, the buffering effect of trees is lost, and the damage storms cause to populated regions increases. Each year tropical storms kill at least 20,000 people and cause $8 billion in damage.

Climate control

Tropical forests play a significant role in the regulation of the climate. The immense expanse of vegetation cycles large quantities of water, thereby influencing global climate as well as local and regional precipitation and temperature. Elimination of rainforests can alter the planet's climate in a number of ways. Tropical deforestation contributes up to 30 percent of all the carbon dioxide human beings add to the atmosphere, as well as unknown amounts of methane and nitrous oxide. These gases add to global warming, which threatens agriculture and the quality of life worldwide.

An estimated two-thirds of all the fresh water on Earth is contained in the Amazon Basin alone (excluding water that is frozen in polar ice or trapped underground). This water constantly circulates in a hydrological cycle. The water that falls as rain is absorbed by soil and forest plants. Some water evaporates in the heat, while some is transpired—breathed—back into the atmosphere by the plants. The moisture reforms as clouds and returns again to the Earth as rain. More than half the water in the region cycles back through the system in this manner.

As water in rainforests circulates, it regulates the balance of regional climate, a balance that has been stable for centuries. As deforestation progresses, however, less water remains in the system. Deforestation significantly reduces rainfall and increases surface temperatures in rainforests. The result is a general drying trend that eventually can have broader regional climatic repercussions. Deforestation in the Brazilian Amazon, for example, is expected to alter the climate in the agricultural regions to the south and west of the basin.

Destruction of rainforest cover may also alter global climate patterns. Different types of ground cover absorb or reflect varying amounts of solar radiation. Snow and desert, which are relatively shiny, reflect solar energy into the atmosphere and outer space. Forested areas—especially the dense green forests of the tropics—absorb solar energy. A broad uprising of air follows the rainforest belt around the equator, driven in part by the heat absorbed by tropical forests. This massive equatorial uprising helps drive the circulation patterns of the entire global atmosphere. Tropical deforestation can disrupt this process, altering wind and rainfall patterns worldwide. Predicted consequences include reduced rainfall and disruption of conditions in the grain belts in the northern half of the United States and Canada, as well as in much of Europe and the Soviet Union.

Tropical forests, like all forests, are primarily composed of carbon and nitrogen. The impact of tropical forest clearing on global climate is due primarily to the emission of carbon dioxide, methane, and nitrous oxide caused by combustion or other forms of decomposition. These chemicals absorb the sun's energy and cause a general warming of the atmosphere. This process, called the greenhouse effect, naturally keeps the planet warm enough to sustain life. In the past 100 years, however, gases released by human activities have added to the natural greenhouse effect. The predicted consequences of global warming include rising sea levels, increased storm intensities, altered weather patterns, and forest dieback.

Carbon dioxide plays the largest role; among the various

gases that cause global warming, it is responsible for roughly half the greenhouse effect. Carbon dioxide is created when fossil fuels such as oil, natural gas, and coal are burned to generate electricity, power our cars, or heat our homes. It is also released when forests are cleared and burned. The carbon dioxide content of the Earth's atmosphere has increased by 25 percent over the last 100 to 150 years.

Deforestation of dense, virgin forests is resulting in the release of about 1.4 billion tons of carbon dioxide per year. In addition, deforestation of open forests and regenerating forests is responsible for the release of another 1.1 billion tons. The total release of 2.5 billion tons accounts for about 30 percent of all carbon dioxide emissions from human activities annually.

Concentrations of methane and nitrous oxide are also increasing in the atmosphere, contributing to global warming. The concentration of methane in the atmosphere has doubled over the last century. Emissions of methane from tropical deforestation are estimated to account for 10 to 15 percent of the current increase. The amount of nitrous oxide released has not been estimated.

The destruction and burning of tropical rainforests contribute to the buildup of carbon in the atmosphere. The living plant matter in tropical forests stores vast amounts of carbon dioxide that would otherwise remain in the atmosphere and add to the greenhouse effect. When rainforests are cleared to make room for farms or cattle ranches, the trees and vegetation burned or left to decay emit carbon dioxide and methane into the atmosphere.

The National Academy of Sciences estimates that the temperature of the Earth's atmosphere will increase between 2.7 and 8.1 degrees Fahrenheit in the next 50 to 100 years. Even at the low end of this range, the increase would bring global average temperatures to a level not seen in 6,000 years. At the high end, we would have to adjust, within less than a century, to average temperatures present during the age of the dinosaurs.

RAINMAKER

Rainforests Create Their Own Weather

We've long known that vegetation is determined in part by the climate of a region, but recent scientific studies and computer models of rainforest weather reveal an interesting twist: the weather in tropical rainforests is in part determined by the vegetation growing there.

This phenomenon has strong repercussions when it comes to deforestation. If too much forest is cleared, the weather in the region can change, making reforestation impossible.

Using supercomputers and a mathematical model of the climate, researchers have concluded that turning the South American rainforest into cattle pasture will reduce rainfall in the region by 25 percent and will increase average temperatures in the area by 5 degrees Fahrenheit. The dry season will also lengthen.

Evaporation of water from plants and soil may account for half of all the water that falls on the Amazon rainforest. As the plants are removed from the system, the cycle is disrupted and less water is retained. The result is a general drying trend that may make the area inhospitable for future plant growth.

The probability of more frequent and intense droughts will increase with the buildup of greenhouse gases. One government model predicts that the number of days above 95 degrees Fahrenheit in the U.S. corn belt will triple if the average temperature rises only three degrees globally. Reduced crop yields would result. A one- to two-foot rise in sea level caused by global warming would force salt water into coastal drinking water systems and cause massive, sudden, and violent changes in the economy and usability of shorelines nationwide. For example, coastal cities like Miami would need more storm sewers, if not dikes, to keep the sea at bay. Much of the nation's wetlands, like those along the Mississippi Delta, would be inundated, threatening the spawning grounds for a multi-billion-dollar commercial fishery and shellfishery.

Part of the world strategy for cutting emissions of greenhouse gases will be to convince developing countries to take greater strides to reduce loss of their tropical forests. But our own current logging practices in Washington, Oregon, and Alaska and our reluctance to preserve the last small fraction of old-growth forest and associated biological diversity eliminate any credibility we might have in seeking cooperation from tropical countries.

These countries are very much aware of the example we set. In 1989, the general secretary of Brazil's Foreign Ministry, Paulo Tarso Flecha de Lima, noted that "the developed countries are not the most prodigious examples when it comes to the environment." Reforming our own government's forestry policies is essential to our having any influence with the governments of the rainforest countries.

Covenant of the ark

Tropical forests provide the planet with much of its biological diversity, or biodiversity—the enormous gene pool that nature depends on for survival. Every rainforest species is a living repository of an immense amount of genetic information, the building blocks of life. This large and diverse gene pool ensures a healthy, balanced ecosystem. It allows the natural selection process to take place—the keystone of evolution, and hence of the successful continuation of a species. By being able to draw upon a vast and varied gene pool, species can adapt and reproduce in response to environmental pressures such as changing climatic conditions and disease.

Diversity gives nature its resilience to change. The climatic changes that are expected to occur in the near future due to global warming will place unanticipated stresses on forest ecosystems. The greater the biological diversity represented in these systems, the greater chance these systems will have to adapt to climatic change.

Tragically, the planet's gene pool is suffering huge losses as habitat destruction pushes more and more species over the brink of extinction. Scientists estimate that up to 17,000 species a year are made extinct as tropical rainforests are destroyed.

All species are bound together by a complex web of relationships and interdependencies. For example, insects pollinate a large variety of plants. The plants, in turn, provide food for numerous herbivorous animals and other insects. Herbivores and insects provide a source of food for carnivorous mammals and birds. These animals keep prey populations in check and recycle nutrients to the plants through their waste.

Alterations of any of these processes will be felt throughout the ecosystem, depending on the complexity of the flora and fauna relationships. As a result, no one knows which, if any, species are expendable. Picture them as rivets on an airplane. You can probably remove a few and the plane will continue to fly, but take away enough and the wings will surely fall off. The question is, just how many are needed to keep the plane aloft?

Extinction of species is nothing new on this planet. Sixty-five million years ago, 60 to 80 percent of the species of life on Earth vanished. Although the exact cause of that mass extinction is unknown, we do know why extinction is taking place today. In the immortal words of cartoon character Pogo, "We have met the enemy, and it is us."

The earlier great extinction differs from the current spasm. It is believed that many more species of plants are being destroyed this time around, something scientists consider very troubling for the future of all species. The implications of this fact are far graver than the extinction that signaled the end of the

Thanks, turkey

The seed of the beautiful *Calvaria* tree refused to germinate for years, leading botanists to speculate that it needed to be eaten by the now-extinct dodo which, like the *Calvaria*, originated on the island of Mauri tius in the Indian Ocean.

No seedlings could be found on the island, only full-grown trees, hundreds of years old. Then a botanist fed some *Calvaria* seeds to a domestic turkey, and after passing through the bird, the seeds sprouted. The trees were saved from extinction.

dinosaurs. Because the cause—human activity—will probably persist, the natural rebound that followed earlier extinctions most likely won't take place. The result, scientists fear, may be as severe as a nuclear winter.

If the majority of species of life on Earth are allowed to perish, it is not clear that humankind will survive. Even if we can survive, our lives in a world depleted of over half its species will surely be impoverished. We will be forever robbed of the foods, the industrial products, and the medicines the rainforests of the world hold in storage for us. Millions of tribal people will lose their home, and their ancient ways will be lost to the world forever. We will have to face a world with an uncertain and changing climate—a world with a shrunken and therefore vulnerable genetic resource base. Clearly, we need to protect tropical rainforests for the sake of all life on Earth.

CHAPTER THREE

When Trees Fall

When Trees Fall

How rainforests are being destroyed

In the minute it takes you to read this page, a piece of tropical forest the size of 10 city blocks will vanish forever. Close to 55,000 square miles of rainforest are being destroyed each year. That's an area the size of the state of New York. Of the 8 million square miles of tropical rainforest that once encircled the equatorial region of the planet, only 3.4 million square miles remain.

The greatest forest losses are occurring in Brazil, Indonesia, and Zaire because these countries still contain the most forested areas. Although there is uncertainty in these estimates, and deforestation rates vary from country to country and from year to year, one trend has remained generally constant: deforestation rates are increasing and have nearly doubled in the last 10 years.

Tropical forests are being cleared for many reasons. Slash-and-burn farmers clear forest to plant crops, ranchers clear forest to create grazing land for cattle, and loggers clear forest to extract timber. Wood gathering for domestic fuel and internationally financed development projects such as mines, highways, and dams also result in the loss of forests. These mechanisms of tropical deforestation are often the result of deeper socioeconomic problems, such as poverty, inequitable land distribution, population growth, and heavy foreign debt.

Economic development that results in deforestation is often both a cause and a consequence of foreign debt. Developing countries borrow money to develop their resources and improve their general standard of living. To pay off the debt that accumulates from that borrowing, countries are forced to pursue rapid and often destructive growth.

Frequently, the justification for economic expansion into the forests is based on gaining short-term profits to fund the debt and doesn't take into account the long-term ecological impact of forest clearing. Nor are all the economic repercussions always considered, such as the loss of nontimber forest products (for example, fruits, nuts, rubber, and medicinal plants) or the loss of both hydroelectric generating capacity and fisheries due to siltation caused by deforestation.

The underlying socioeconomic conditions that drive this problem must be addressed if we are to prevent further tropical deforestation. Responsibility for protecting the world's tropical forests rests not only with the rainforest countries but also with developed countries that have set a poor example of natural-resource stewardship with the clearing of their own temperate forests, high levels of resource consumption, short-sighted investment in developing countries, and provision of markets for tropical forest goods that are not obtained in a manner that sustains resources.

The cattle connection

Cattle ranching has destroyed more rainforest in Central America than any other activity. Some countries in South America have also experienced substantial deforestation as a

Hold the beef

A typical four-ounce hamburger made from rainforest beef involves the destruction of about 55 square feet of tropical forest, an area the size of a small kitchen. Each hamburger represents the destruction of 1,000 pounds of living matter, including 1 large tree, 50 saplings and seedlings representing 20 to 30 different species, thousands of insects of several hundred species, and an almost unimaginable variety of mosses, fungi, and microorganisms.

result of cattle ranching. For example, ranchers converted over 38,000 square miles of Brazilian rainforest to pasture for cattle between 1966 and 1983. In the last 40 years, two-thirds of the primary rainforest of Central America has been cleared, and the number of beef cattle there has more than doubled.

Cattle ranching in tropical countries also intensifies deforestation by forcing peasant farmers into the rainforest to seek new land to farm when they are evicted by ranchers who want to convert their farmland to pasture. This pattern has recurred throughout Central and South America.

Cattle ranching causes the land to decline in quality as the soil becomes depleted of nutrients. In fact, land cleared from rainforests generally supports cattle for only three to seven years before it deteriorates beyond recovery, and rainforest cattle ranches are often only 25 percent as productive as ranches in more temperate regions.

Rainforest cattle ranchers abandon converted pastures once they become useless, and move on to clear more rainforest.

Most of the ranches that were converted from rainforest in the Amazon Basin before 1980 were abandoned by the mid-1980s, and most of the pasture that was converted from rainforest in Costa Rica lies abandoned today because it can no longer support cattle grazing.

Rainforest ranchers have relied on government subsidies and international loans, which make cattle raising artificially profitable. In the past, the World Bank and the Inter-American Development Bank have promoted cattle ranching in rainforest regions by giving substantial loans for that purpose; these two banks made almost $4 billion in loans and grants for cattle raising in the rainforest during the 1970s. Rainforest governments have also supported cattle ranching with land giveaways, tax breaks, and free technical assistance. Without this support, rainforest ranching would lose much of its appeal.

Some of the Central American beef exports wind up in the United States, where they are often less expensive than domestic beef. In 1988 the United States imported almost 50,000 tons of beef and veal, worth almost $1 billion, from Central American countries. The majority of the imports came from Costa Rica, Guatemala, and Honduras. These imports accounted for only 7 percent of our total beef and veal purchases worldwide.

Importing countries pay more for rainforest beef than

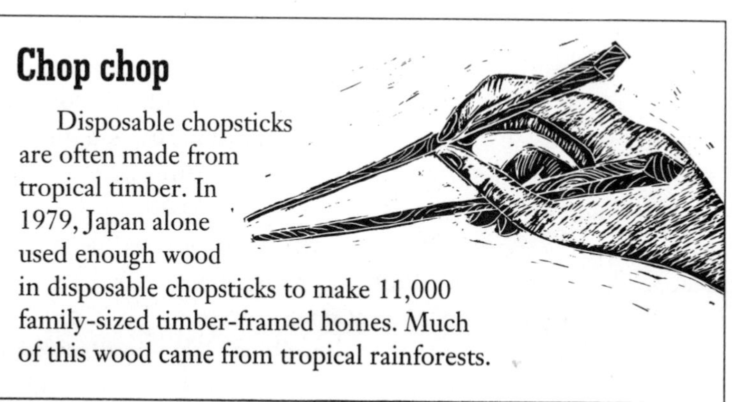

Chop chop

Disposable chopsticks are often made from tropical timber. In 1979, Japan alone used enough wood in disposable chopsticks to make 11,000 family-sized timber-framed homes. Much of this wood came from tropical rainforests.

consumers in the exporting countries can afford. Although their beef exports have tripled in the last 25 years, the people of Costa Rica, El Salvador, Guatemala, and Nicaragua eat less beef now than they did 25 years ago because they cannot match the prices paid by importing countries like the United States. In fact, according to Catherine Caufield, author of *In the Rainforest*, the average pet cat in the United States eats more beef in a year than the average person in Costa Rica.

In some countries, reducing trade in tropical beef may ease some of the pressure to clear rainforests for cattle ranching. However, it will also have potentially severe economic effects on countries that can ill afford to suffer them. To reduce the impact of cattle ranching on tropical forests we must persuade governments in Central and South America to discourage cattle ranching, and we must get the international banks and development agencies to direct lending toward projects that will provide long-term economic support and contribute to debt reduction.

A clear-cut problem

Tropical hardwoods are valued for their beauty, strength, and durability. Resistant to wear, rot, and insect damage, hardwoods make excellent wall paneling, floorboards, and furniture. These characteristics have led to demand for tropical hardwoods in developed countries, including the United States. Tropical hardwoods also make their way into paper, packaging, and other uses for which alternative woods are equally suitable. For example, Japan uses much of its tropical hardwood imports for disposable molds that hold concrete during construction and are then thrown away.

While Japan imports primarily unprocessed logs, the United States is the leading importer of processed tropical timber. Plywood, lumber, and veneer account for almost all tropical hardwood imports, although we also import some hardwood logs and manufactured items such as furniture, tableware, and musical instruments. Certain tropical tree species make excellent thin plywoods, less than one-quarter inch thick, ideal for interior wall paneling and hollow-core doors. Hardwood lumber used for construction represents another leading use of tropical wood in the United States.

Veneer is the name for very thin sheets of wood that are used to make plywood and paneling, the latter particularly for use in recreational vehicles. Veneer coating is popular for furniture such as bookshelves, tables, and desks, and veneer is also used, like plywood, to make hollow-core doors. About 40 percent of hardwood veneer comes from tropical countries.

In addition to the traditional uses for hardwoods, new technologies allow manufacturers to make paper and paper products, such as packaging materials and paper cups and plates, from rainforest hardwoods. Until recently, most wood pulp was made from softwoods, which generally come from temperate forests. New chipping machines now enable manufacturers to make pulp and paper products from rainforest hardwoods. The new machines can reduce an entire 150-foot hardwood tree, leaves and all, to a pile of poker-chip-sized pieces in a few minutes. They have opened up a new use for rainforest trees, thus increasing demand for the wood. Take Papua New Guinea for example. In 1974, it exported no wood chips, but by the mid-1980s that small country was exporting almost 15 million cubic feet of chips per year.

Commercial logging has cut a wide swath through the world's tropical forests. Not only has excessive tropical forest logging contributed to species extinction and the long-term loss of income to rainforest countries, it has caused severe human difficulties as well. In many countries different laws govern the land itself; underground resources, such as minerals, coal, and oil; and above-ground resources, such as timber. Often, legal claims by communities to local forests have been challenged by loggers who have been given legal title to the timber resources by the government.

RAINFOREST HERO

Francisco "Chico" Mendes Filho

December 15, 1944 to December 22, 1988

Chico Mendes was born in the Seringal Cachoeira, a part of the Brazilian rainforest rich with wild rubber trees.

Many of the 300,000 rubber tappers in Brazil live in the state of Acre, near the border of Peru and Bolivia in the far western region of Amazonia. Chico grew up among the rubber tappers; his family had been in the trade for generations.

In 1969 the Brazilian government began its National Integration Program, a costly road-building and colonization program designed to secure the disputed territories in the heart of the rainforest. Huge incentives were offered to relocate some of the millions of poor people from the more populated eastern region of the country and to attract large investors to establish cattle ranches in the rainforest.

As the ranchers and settlers came to clear the rainforest in Acre, the rubber tappers were forced to relocate. Most just left the forest as they were instructed. Chico Mendes refused. He told his people they had rights, and he began to organize them to resist the relocations.

Chico had never heard of Martin Luther King or Mahatma Gandhi, but the idea of nonviolent resistance came to him naturally. He thought up a plan for a nonviolent blockade, a line of 200 to 300 families of rubber tappers to block the bulldozers that were coming to clear the forest. In 13 years Chico organized 45 blockades and is said to have saved close to 3 million acres of forest.

Chico set up the Rural Workers' Union and was elected town councilman in Xapuri. His life was threatened many times.

Over the next several

Chico Mendes

continued from previous page

years, Chico rose to international prominence as an opponent of the destruction of the Amazon. As an alternative to roads and ranches, Chico lobbied in favor of "extractive reserves," areas set aside for sustainable use by rubber tappers and gatherers of nuts, fruits, and fibers. About 5 million acres have now been set aside as extractive reserves in Brazil or are planned to be set aside.

One of the extractive reserves Chico helped to establish by use of blockade and lobbying was in the Seringal Cachoeira, the forest where he was born and raised. The land had been claimed by Darli Alves, a local rancher accredited with dozens of murders. Darli had vowed to kill Chico.

In December of 1988, Chico went to the town of Sena Madureira, deep in the forest, to enlist 500 more tappers for the union. He returned home on December 22, three days before Christmas. That evening, as he was stepping out of the kitchen door into his backyard, Chico was blasted by a 20-gauge shotgun at close range. He was dead within minutes.

Darci Alves, the 21-year-old son of the rancher Darli, confessed to the killing. Darci may have pulled the trigger, but according to writer Alex Shoumatoff, Darci almost certainly was acting on orders from his father. Darli belonged to an organization of wealthy landowners known as the Rural Democratic Union.

Chico Mendes is survived by his wife, Ilza, and their two children, Elenira and Sandino.

Contributions for the continuation of Chico Mendes's work, and for the support of his family, can be sent to the following address:

The Chico Mendes Fund
Environmental Defense Fund
257 Park Avenue South
New York, NY 10010

In Bolivia, Guaraní Indians who fought to obtain legal title to the land under one law were confronted by loggers who had been given timber concessions to the same land under a different law. This is permissible under the existing Bolivian legal structure, making it very difficult for local communities to gain control over their own forest resources.

The lack of local control has led to overcutting of many tropical forests. Africa was once the leading source of tropical hardwoods to the developed world, but overcutting there has depleted the majority of rainforests, and few remain productive. In Ghana and the Ivory Coast, for example, logging is one of the causes that have brought about the loss of up to 80 percent of the original rainforest. Gabon has already lost over 60 percent of its original primary rainforest cover, and logging concessions have been granted in three-fourths of the forests that remain.

Southeast Asia has eclipsed Africa as the leading supplier of tropical hardwood to the international market, but its rainforests, too, are becoming widely decimated by logging. Over 80 percent of Thailand's primary rainforest has been destroyed or severely damaged.

Recent studies show that timber harvesting can result in the loss of valuable economic revenue because of its impact on fisheries, tourism, and the loss of products that could have been extracted sustainably, such as nuts, fruits, latex, and oils. Deforestation has increased the sediment load of many tropical rivers, causing declines in both freshwater and saltwater fisheries. An economic analysis of the effects of logging versus fishing and tourism in Palawan in the Philippines found that a logging ban would save more than $11 million over 10 years, even taking into account the revenues from the logging operations.

A flood exacerbated by deforestation that left hundreds dead in November 1988 finally convinced the Thai government to ban all commercial logging. Subsequent developments in Thailand underscore the difficulty of enforcing a timber ban. Loggers have managed to circumvent the Thai ban by cutting trees near the Laos and Myanmar (Burma) borders, taking the logs across the borders, and then importing them back into Thailand, as though they had originated in Laos or Myanmar.

Indonesia, once a minor player in the tropical hardwoods market, now exports more hardwood plywood than any other country. By 1988 Indonesia was exporting over $3 billion worth of hardwood plywood annually; only oil generated more export earnings. Diminishing timber reserves led the Indonesian government to impose a ban on raw log exports in 1985. The ban has not been enforced, however. In the first five months of 1989, Indonesia exported nearly $1 million worth of tropical hardwood logs to the United States.

The Philippines, with less than 10 percent of its original forest cover remaining, also has banned timber exports. Malaysia banned raw-log exports from its mainland rainforest in 1985, but it still exports wood from its provinces of Sarawak and Sabah on the island of Borneo. The rainforests of these two provinces are the oldest in the world, but they may be gone in as little as seven years. Loggers there have access to 95 percent of the rainforest not already set aside in existing or proposed reserves. Japan, the world's largest consumer of tropical timber, takes most of the rainforest wood cut in Sarawak and Sabah; close to 90 percent of Japanese log imports comes from the two Malaysian states. Japan's voracious appetite for tropical timber is also responsible for the deforestation of large sectors of rainforest in Thailand, Indonesia, and the Philippines.

As reserves in Southeast Asia dwindle, timber companies are turning to even more remote rainforests, such as those in Papua New Guinea. There is also increasing interest in Latin American timber, and the region is poised for a great expansion in logging. In three months in 1987, Brazil alone exported more mahogany lumber to the United States than to all other countries combined for any 12-month period in the previous 10 years. The other important tropical timber producers in Latin America are Paraguay, Ecuador, Colombia, and Peru.

TWO PROJECTS IN BRAZIL

Fostering Deforestation

Two massive development programs in Brazil illustrate how financing from international funding agencies such as the World Bank and the International Monetary Fund foster deforestation. One-third of all the remaining tropical rainforest in the world is in Brazil, most of it in the Amazon Basin. Yet deforestation in this region is proceeding at a very rapid rate. The main culprits are two government-sponsored development programs, Polonoroeste and Grande Carajas.

Polonoroeste is a highway and resettlement program in the western states of Rondonia and Matto Grosso, which have a combined area of 160,000 square miles. The program is designed to alleviate overpopulation problems in southern Brazil. Its centerpiece is a highway, BR-364, which the Brazilian government cut into Rondonia in 1970 to open the region to settlers. Polonoroeste has made Rondonia the area with the most rapid deforestation in Brazil; 20 percent of its rainforest has already vanished, and at the present rate of destruction the rest will be gone within 25 years.

Until 1970 Rondonia and Matto Grosso were mostly undeveloped and inaccessible, but with construction of BR-364 a flood of immigration began. Rondonia's population doubled in the 1980s and has now passed 1.2 million. Many of the colonists in Rondonia and Matto Grosso become slash-and-burn farmers, but because the poor soil dooms this agricultural method to failure, they are often forced to sell their land to speculators soon after clearing it. Then they move on. Those who do not sell willingly are often driven out. Violence and bloodshed are common. Life in the rainforest is hardly an improvement for most of the newcomers. Health care for

Fostering Deforestation
continued from previous page

the settlers and education for their young are lacking; there were 240,000 reported cases of malaria in 1987, and 200,000 children in Rondonia don't go to school because there are no schools in the state. According to Brazilian business analysts, if it weren't for government incentives and price supports for cocoa and other crops, no one would farm Rondonia.

The Grande Carajas program is a mining and mineral development scheme designed to exploit Brazil's extensive mineral deposits of iron, copper, nickel, and bauxite. The $3.5 billion program, which encompasses over 300,000 square miles, includes smelters to convert iron ore into pig iron. The smelters are fired by charcoal which is made by burning rainforest trees. One acre of dense forest supplies only enough charcoal to fuel an iron smelter for about two hours. The project has already destroyed close to two-thirds of the trees in the state of Minas Gerais.

At the present pace of timber extraction, the revenues generated by commercial logging will be short-lived, however. Currently, the tropical timber trade produces roughly $6 billion annually for tropical countries. That figure is expected to drop to $2 billion by the turn of the century as supplies shrink due to poorly managed logging. By the year 2000, many tropical countries will be forced to become net timber importers.

This need not be the case. Alternatives to typical clear-cutting practices, such as selective logging and small-patch clear-cutting, can lead to sustainable timber harvesting. In selective logging, only the commercially desirable species are removed from a patch of forest. Out of the thousands of tropical hardwood species, only a few are sought after by commercial buyers.

Southeast Asia, for example, exports only about two dozen of its thousands of types of trees. By leaving most of the trees standing, selective loggers can preserve the integrity of the ecosystem and allow the rainforest to survive. Even so, most loggers clear-cut entire areas of forest and either burn undesirable species or leave them to rot.

Selective logging often creates its own problems, however. Because of the density of the trees and the vast entanglement of climbing plants and vines that wind from one tree to another, a falling tree can damage or destroy dozens of other trees. When the loggers drag the selected trees to the road, extensive soil damage results. A commercial logging operation using selective logging techniques may leave up to two-thirds of the remaining trees damaged, and almost a third of the soil left bare and permanently harmed. If care is taken to cut climbing plants and vines loose before trees are felled, and if trees are cut to fall at angles that will minimize the number of other trees they damage on the way down, much of this destruction can be avoided.

Another problem with selective logging is high-grading—the impoverishment of the forest through the removal of all the valuable species. Care must be taken to leave examples of some of the valuable species behind to serve as a source of seeds for forest regeneration. Selective logging also takes more time, thus raising the cost of logging. Given the right conditions, however, selective logging might be successful.

Small-patch clear-cutting is another promising technique for protecting the rainforest. Using this approach, loggers clear a small patch of forest but leave the surrounding areas intact. Natural forest growth eventually fills the holes back in, reseeding the patch with local species. Disruptions to wildlife, watershed, and climate are thereby minimized.

The Palacazu Rural Development Project in the Peruvian Amazon illustrates the potential of small-scale strip clear-cutting. In this project, the forests are collectively managed and owned by local indigenous people. The timber is all processed locally, retaining much of its value within the community.

The community has devoted about half of its managed portion of the forest to long, narrow clear-cut strips. This pattern mimics natural gap formations, which are the means by which these forests typically regenerate in the absence of human harvesting. Nearby primary forest provides the seeds for natural regeneration of hundreds of species. The technique, while relatively new, provides a promising means of sustainably harvesting timber while conserving the integrity of the ecosystem.

Cartón de Colombia has successfully used the small-patch clear-cutting technique to log its 200-square-mile concession on Colombia's Pacific coast. Lifting trees out with ropes to avoid soil damage, the operation has cleared about 3,000 acres a year. The forest has regenerated well, and observers claim the older second growth looks like primary forest.

Despite careful management, parcels are still vulnerable to devastation. Landless colonists or timber poachers often follow new roads into previously inaccessible areas and destroy vast tracts of forest. Managers of the Cartón de Colombia project discovered settlers cutting the second growth on the small-patch clear-cuts before the trees had time to mature, thus reducing the chances for forest recovery.

Unfortunately, neither selective logging nor small-patch clear-cutting is widely practiced. So far the idea of sustainable tropical forestry has proven to be elusive. According to the International Tropical Timber Organization (ITTO), sustainable tropical forestry has succeeded on less than one-eighth of 1 percent of all tropical forests. Worldwide, such efforts have had "negligible" success, according to ITTO.

A third technique being tried to reduce the pressure to cut timber from the virgin forests is the creation of tree plantations. These tree farms are designed to supply timber for domestic demand as well as export. Brazil has established almost 10 million acres of tree plantations over a 20-year period. In the process, the country has gone from being a net importer of pulp and paper products to exporting $365 million worth of plantation-grown products a year. In Southeast Asia, about 200,000 acres of hardwood plantations are established each year.

The trouble with plantations is that many growers clear the primary forest to start their projects, using the profits from the felled native timber to offset start-up costs. For example, in Ecuador and Colombia, there has been large-scale clearing of tropical forest for oil palm plantations. In another case, the Scott Paper Company planned to clear over 300,000 acres of primary rainforest on the Indonesian Province of Irian Jaya to create a tree plantation and pulp mill for producing tissue and toilet paper. In addition to its ecological consequences, the project would have affected the traditional homelands of over 40,000 people. Public opposition eventually convinced the company to drop the idea, at least for now.

Social and economic disruption of local communities can be severe. In Karnataka, India, for example, rural communities were not allowed on common lands after the establishment of eucalyptus plantations, and this lack of access reduced their supply of fuelwood and fodder. The project, which required little labor, provided support to few in the communities. Rural poor in Karnataka eventually protested the plantations by uprooting the eucalyptus seedlings.

There are other problems with tree plantations. One important consequence is the loss of biological diversity and general ecosystem simplification. In cases where only one or a few species are planted, the trees become much more vulnerable to pest infestation, disease, and environmental change. Species diversity provides the genetic resources to adapt to environmental alterations and restricts the progress of fungal diseases and insects. There are numerous instances of tree plantations suffering massive losses from insect attack.

In degraded rainforest areas natural regeneration should be encouraged instead of tree plantations. Where the land has been severely degraded, regeneration should be undertaken by

Flower power

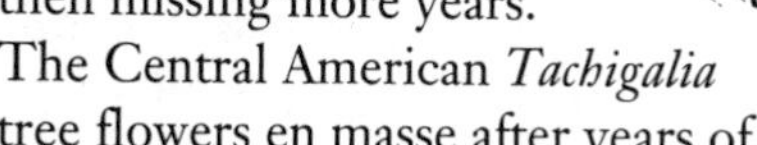

The flowering cycles of most rainforest trees remain a mystery to scientists. Most trees seem to flower without any obvious pattern, missing years at a time, then flowering again, then missing more years. The Central American *Tachigalia* tree flowers en masse after years of lying dormant, then dies. In the rainforests of Malaysia and Indonesia, nearly all the trees, comprising many different species, flower in unison, sometimes for areas of hundreds of square miles. Some trees will produce 4 million flowers, over 650,000 in a single day.

planting a large variety of native species to provide diversity and wildlife habitat.

The challenge is for tropical timber importers to design a system that rewards and thereby encourages sustainable forest management without crippling tropical economies. We must encourage the companies and government officials who regulate and exploit the tropical hardwoods trade to reduce the level of cutting and to perform timber harvesting in a more ecologically sound fashion. Our ultimate goal must be that rainforest hardwoods only be taken from sustainably managed forests.

In the long run, tropical forestry projects will neither be sustainable nor provide substantial benefit to local communities until legal control over forest resources is placed in the hands of the local communities. Only in this way will those managing the forests have a stake in their long-term health and sustainability;

only then will the financial revenues benefit local economies.

One way the United States can promote this outcome is through the wise use of market influence. Consumers of tropical hardwoods must seek to determine the origin of hardwoods and purchase only those that come from well-managed systems. Identification could be made easy through the imposition of labeling requirements by our government and the governments of importing countries.

At the same time, the federal government should be encouraged to restrict imports of both processed and unprocessed tropical hardwoods except from countries and operations that meet the criteria of sustainability. This could be accomplished through the establishment of a tariff system, where countries that demonstrated progress toward sustainable forestry would be rewarded with lower tariffs or no tariff restrictions. Among the criteria for favorable tariff treatment must be control by communities over local forests and their resources, including the planning and implementation of timber sales and forest management; forestry projects that don't displace or interfere with local land tenants and that protect the land rights of native tribes; and timber harvesting that does not result in significant soil erosion, loss of biological diversity, or decreased forest productivity.

Beating trees into plowshares

Small-scale farming is another major cause of tropical deforestation. In fact, small-scale farmers clear about half the total rainforest lost each year. Like the pioneers who migrated to the western United States in the nineteenth century, many farmers come to the rainforest to pursue the dream of a better life. Attracted by well-publicized government campaigns promising free land and generous tax incentives, rainforest settlers come ready to build a future with their hands and to tame a wilderness. Most are forced into the rainforest by poverty, landlessness, and, in the case of Indonesia, relocation projects. But newcomers to the rainforest quickly discover that rainforest soils support crops for only a few years. They are forced into continuous migration in search of new patches of forest to clear. For most, the dream of sustainable farming remains just that—a dream. For the wildlife dependent upon undisturbed rainforest habitat for survival, the encroachment of farming is a nightmare.

Historically, indigenous tribal farmers in the rainforest have typically used a technique called shifting cultivation. A shifting cultivator cuts down and burns most of the trees in a small patch of forest, along with whatever underbrush and ground cover grows there. Burning releases nutrients stored in the vegetation and makes these nutrients—in the form of ash—available to the crops that are planted on the cleared ground.

The benefits of being able to grow and harvest edible crops are short term, however. Burning damages the root mat and disturbs organic matter in the soil, increasing erosion. Clearing the forest exposes the soil to the direct impact of heavy tropical rains and accelerates nutrient leaching. It also releases carbon dioxide, methane, and nitrous oxide—dangerous greenhouse gases—to the atmosphere.

Cleared forest areas can support only one or two years' worth of crop cultivation before the loss of nutrients and weed encroachment prevent further production. Once this stage has been reached, shifting cultivators abandon the plot so that the forest can reestablish itself. However, forest regeneration is possible only if there is intact forest nearby to serve as a source of seeds, if the soil has not become too impoverished and compacted, and if enough time is allowed for the forest to mature. In the past, patches that were cleared were small, and the land was given sufficient time to reforest.

Shifting cultivation has been practiced for thousands of years and, until recently, the world's tropical forests remained fairly resilient to the technique. That's because the method was

OIL IN THE AMAZON

Polluting the Rainforest

The extraction of oil, gold, and other minerals poses a serious threat to the health of tropical forests and indigenous peoples. These activities frequently release toxic chemicals into the forest, contaminating land and poisoning streams, rivers, and groundwater.

In the Brazilian Amazon, for example, liquid mercury used by miners to separate gold from raw ore washes into streams and rivers, causing serious health hazards to the local Indians, the miners themselves, and local flora and fauna. In Papua New Guinea, gold and copper mining are not only denuding immense sections of the rainforest but also creating a mountain of tailings—waste material contaminated with toxic substances.

Oil development by local and international oil companies in the Ecuadorian Amazon, known locally as the Oriente, has caused considerable degradation of the forest. Local authorities say air, water, and soil contamination by petroleum facilities is widespread and severe. Waste oil and contaminated muds and water from the drilling process are often discharged directly into surrounding streams or into open pits. The toxic chemicals contaminate drinking water and enter the food chain, killing fish and wildlife.

Petroleum wastes and natural gas byproducts are typically burned directly into the air, producing air pollutants that kill nearby vegetation and cause respiratory problems among workers and neighboring communities. Spills at well sites and from pipelines are common. Ruptures in Ecuador's main pipeline system have dumped nearly 17 million gallons of oil into the rivers and soils of the Amazon.

The impacts of petro-

Polluting

continued from previous page

leum development in the Oriente threaten the health and welfare of local indigenous populations. New diseases have been introduced into indigenous communities, traditional sources of food and water have been contaminated or destroyed, sacred areas have been desecrated; and conflict has flared with colonists and speculators who follow the oil company roads into indigenous lands.

Over 1.5 million acres of rainforest in Ecuador are currently being exploited for oil production. Another 7.5 million acres are currently under exploration, and concessions for an additional 6 million acres are expected. Much of this activity is taking place within established national parks, wildlife reserves, and the traditional lands of indigenous peoples. The World Bank and several multinational oil companies, including Texaco, Conoco, Arco, Unocal, Occidental, and PetroCanada, are key players in this activity. The World Bank is currently considering a $100 million loan to support further exploration and exploitation.

Ecuadorian environmental and indigenous peoples organizations have strongly criticized petroleum development in the Amazon, particularly the involvement of foreign oil companies. A coalition of 13 environmental organizations is now demanding that the government of Ecuador stop all oil development within the boundaries of national parks, conduct rigorous environmental studies of all planned development, and respect the land claims of the Amazonian indigenous peoples.

In addition to Ecuador and other countries in the Amazon, multinational oil companies are now penetrating the forests of Myanmar (Burma), Indonesia, Zaire, Zimbabwe, and Papua New Guinea, among others.

primarily practiced by indigenous rainforest cultures that had low population densities. Fewer people meant less pressure on the forest. The cleared patches of land were allowed to regenerate for many years before being cleared again. So widespread was shifting cultivation in historic times that some observers speculate that every patch of rainforest in the entire Amazon Basin was cultivated at one time or another.

In recent years, however, higher population densities have made shifting cultivation unsustainable. The huge number of farmers who have descended upon the rainforests have placed too much pressure on the land. Not enough time is being given to cleared patches for the forest to regenerate. This "slash-and-burn" farming has replaced traditional, sustainable, shifting cultivation in most tropical forests. As a result, the land in many parts of the globe has become increasingly impoverished and unable to support agriculture for any length of time. Farmers have no choice but to push farther into undeveloped areas of the forest. Inevitably, more trees are cleared.

The rainforest is especially unsuited to the kind of large-scale agriculture practiced in the United States and Europe. Rainforest crops grown on a large scale are highly vulnerable to pests and diseases that flourish in the hot, wet climate. Large cultivated fields provide prime breeding and feeding grounds for insect pests, allowing them to reach damaging proportions.

Some measures can be undertaken to mitigate the impact of slash-and-burn farming on forests. Even so, most such measures will not result in truly long-term sustainable agriculture.

One such measure is agroforestry. It combines techniques of agriculture and forestry on a single plot of land; a farmer plants trees in the same fields as food crops. Planting trees on pastureland or among agricultural crops can provide many benefits, including timber, fuel, fruits and nuts, food for cattle, and fertilizer. Appropriate tree species can shelter food crops and animals from the wind and sun, enrich the soil, prevent erosion, and help the soil retain water. For example, alley cropping uses hedgerows to restore nutrients to the soil and allows croplands to be used on a continuous basis. A farmer practicing alley cropping plants rows of nitrogen-fixing trees and plants, called legumes, between rows of food crops; the leaf litter from the hedgerows becomes fertilizer, while the hedges help stabilize the soil against erosion due to wind and rain. One alley-cropping project in Africa produced a yield of grain four times greater than the average of a non-alley-cropped plot.

Agroforestry has recently gained recognition as an important alternative to shifting cultivation, and agroforestry projects are under way in approximately 100 developing countries. Kenya, for example, now meets 47 percent of its wood needs from agricultural lands, taking pressure off primary forests and increasing the value and productivity of farmland.

Intercropping, the practice of growing a variety of crops together in one field, improves crop yields, protects plants from insect pests, and helps maintain or even improve the soil quality in the farmed area. These multispecies gardens, generally smaller than five acres, can supply a subsistence farm family with all its food, fuel, animal feed, and fiber needs.

Indigenous rainforest peoples have used intercropping methods for thousands of years, with impressive results. Groups in Thailand, New Guinea, Mexico, and the Philippines continue to grow literally hundreds of crops in their small garden-farms, sometimes producing 50 or more food crops at one time from a two-acre plot.

Where intercropping has been introduced to new areas, the results have also been impressive. Farmers in Rwanda have replaced shifting cultivation with intercropped farms, and their harvests have produced over 50 percent more calories, 31 percent more protein, and 62 percent more carbohydrates than single-crop plots of the same size.

These measures will extend the productive life of the land but in most cases will not result in a sustainable system of tropical agriculture. Most tropical forest soils are not suited to agriculture of any kind because they cannot retain nutrients efficiently. This makes the goal of returning to some form of sustainable tropical forest agriculture currently out of reach. In the long run, population densities must be reduced before the tropical forests can provide sustainable support to human populations.

The population bomb

An exploding population has placed untold pressure on the world's rainforests. These pressures are expected to get much more severe in the future. In Indonesia and Brazil, burgeoning populations have led governments to initiate transmigration projects to relocate people from densely populated areas into sparsely populated forests, thus accelerating deforestation. Throughout Asia, Africa, and Latin America growing population densities among the rural poor have sharply increased the pressures to clear forest for crop production and have led to unsustainable agricultural practices. Borrowing for transmigration projects, roads, and electricity generating plants to support growing populations has resulted in rapid and unsustainable development of natural resources to pay back the loans.

The world today contains about 5.3 billion people, and that number is increasing exponentially. Developing countries alone accounted for over 3.6 billion in 1985. The total world population will double in the next 39 years if measures are not taken to reduce the growth rate.

An old French riddle best illustrates the speed and impact of population growth. A pond weed doubles itself in size each day. To cover the pond totally will take 30 days. "The question is," the riddle asks, "how much of the pond will be covered in 29 days?" The answer, of course, is that just half the pond will be covered in 29 days. The weed will then double once more and cover the entire pond the next day.

Most of the future growth in world population is expected

to occur in developing countries, many of which are tropical. This growth, particularly among the rural poor, will accelerate the pressure to clear the forest. In many cases, sustainable forest product extraction is not sufficient to meet the minimum needs of the rural poor because population densities are so great. To obtain a subsistence-level existence, rural populations are forced to "mine" the forest; they remove forest products or clear forest for agriculture faster than the resource can renew itself.

Perhaps one of the most effective investments that could be made in tropical countries to prevent deforestation is to fund access to birth control throughout Africa, Asia, and Latin America. Current world spending on population control is about $3.2 billion. An investment of $9 billion to $10 billion per year is needed to provide access to birth control for 75 percent of the 880 million couples that will be of reproductive age in the year 2000.

Although this may seem like an enormous sum of money, consider that it represents only 3 to 4 percent of all annual development assistance, compared with the 1.2 percent of assistance that presently goes to population control. Nevertheless, U.S. spending on international population control efforts has declined in recent years. In fact, the United States has not contributed to the United Nations Fund for Population Activities since 1985.

Of politics and power

Development projects such as dams, mines, and highways have a devastating impact on large areas of rainforest. Dams flood the primary forest, displace indigenous peoples, and wipe out wildlife. Mining projects degrade the forest and create demand for timber to fuel the smelters. Highways and roads cut by oil and gas exploration teams open the forest to waves of timber poachers or farmers.

Our tax dollars have fueled many of these destructive development programs in tropical forest countries through financing made available by the World Bank and other international financial institutions. Projects are also funded by private donors. The United States is a leading member of a handful of these institutions which, led by the World Bank, have substantial influence over the decisions of governments throughout the world. The World Bank and the regional banks, called multilateral development banks for Africa, Asia, and Latin America, lend roughly $30 billion each year to Third World governments and private enterprises for a wide variety of development projects.

In three of its largest borrowing countries—India, Brazil, and Indonesia—the World Bank has supported massive rural development programs that have needlessly destroyed millions of acres of tropical forests, created terrible health hazards for indigenous peoples and incoming settlers, and forced hundreds of thousands of families to abandon their homes and villages. The World Bank supports logging operations in many borrowing countries with little attention to forest conservation or preservation of biological diversity.

Public involvement and action have had a major impact on the environmental quality of World Bank policies and projects. In many countries, indigenous people and nongovernmental organizations have worked diligently to reform policies. As a result of increasing public pressure, World Bank president Barber Conable declared in 1987 that the Bank would begin to pay greater attention to the environment. Since Conable's speech the Bank has made some small progress in bringing environmental concerns into the selection, preparation, and execution of projects.

However, much more needs to be done. In 1988, environmentalists discovered that the Bank was planning to lend $500 million to Brazil's national power company. Among other things, these funds would help finance the construction of up to 79 new dams in the Amazon and, for the first time in the Bank's

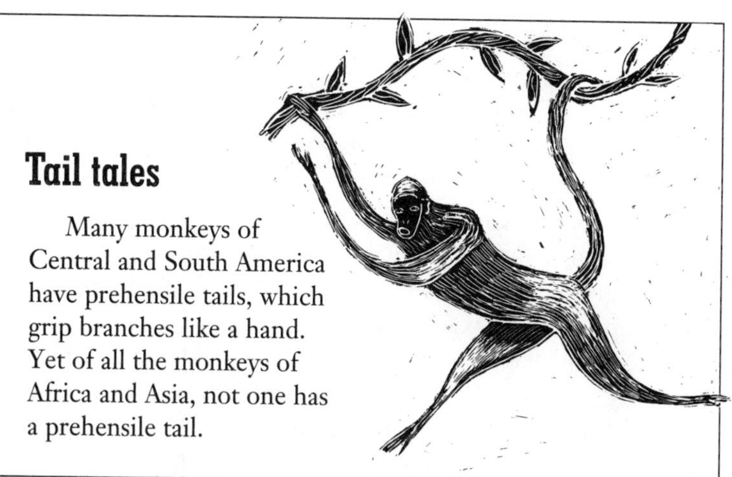

Tail tales

Many monkeys of Central and South America have prehensile tails, which grip branches like a hand. Yet of all the monkeys of Africa and Asia, not one has a prehensile tail.

history, support the development of nuclear power. Only after loud protests from environmentalists in Brazil and the United States did the Bank insist that Brazil withdraw its proposal for the loan. Similarly, in June 1989, environmentalists from Sri Lanka and the United States succeeded in reforming a $20 million World Bank forestry project.

Unfortunately, these encouraging developments must be read against a larger background. The Bank continues to fund a number of environmentally detrimental programs in India, Indonesia, Brazil, and other countries despite angry protests from local communities. While a fire necessitating a hook and ladder company has raged out of control, the Bank has responded with a watering can. This is "greenspeak"—talking a good line on the environment without closing the gap between rhetoric and policy.

In theory, Bank activity in forestry and rural development is intended to meet basic human needs and eliminate poverty among the poorest of the poor in the Third World. In practice, these programs have not differed substantially from other Bank-supported activities. In Brazil and Indonesia, for instance, wealthy landholders, logging companies, and companies from developed nations often benefit at the expense of poor communities, especially indigenous peoples.

There is an urgent need for increased international funding and technical support for sustainable economic activities in tropical forests. The World Bank could be a tremendous force for good in this area. However, recent forestry loans to several West African countries indicate that the Bank's growing forestry program will serve only to make the problem worse, rather than support solutions.

The World Bank's lending for power plants has been of particular concern to environmental organizations throughout the world. Energy projects financed by the World Bank have destroyed sensitive and valuable ecosystems, threatened human health, and necessitated the forced resettlement of tens of thousands of poor and powerless families.

Energy is essential to economic development. However, the Third World is facing a little-known "energy crisis" which, due to the high cost of many energy investments and serious constraints on available capital, means that it will be impossible for many developing countries to meet their expected demand for energy in the coming decades strictly through an increased energy supply.

There is a way out of this bind. According to energy specialists, by the year 2020 the world can achieve a universal standard of living beyond that necessary to satisfy basic needs and with little increase in global energy consumption above today's levels. This does not mean limiting access to the energy services necessary for development. Rather, Brazil, India, Costa Rica, and other developing countries can cut the need for growth in their power-generating capacity through investments in state-of-the-art industrial equipment, lighting systems, air conditioners, and other energy-saving appliances. By doing this, they will realize considerable monetary savings in the bargain.

So far, the U.S. government has taken the lead in calls for environmental policy reforms at the World Bank. Because the

United States is the Bank's largest shareholder it has had a major impact. However, many other countries, especially in South America, are resentful of the United States for its substantial influence over the Bank, which is located in Washington, D.C., and is always run by a U.S. citizen. We must encourage citizens of all nations to make an effort to learn more about the Bank and its projects and to urge their elected representatives and government officials to demand change.

Environmental groups throughout the world have begun to agree on a basic agenda for real environmental reform at the World Bank. The emerging consensus agenda for reform centers on one major need: the World Bank must become more accountable to the public and involve citizens as well as nongovernmental organizations in the planning and implementation of its projects. In this way, the Bank can begin to support truly sustainable economic activity in tropical forests that benefits both the environment and local communities.

Burdens of debt

The $1.3 trillion of accumulated debt owed by developing countries has shaped national development priorities and led to unsustainable exploitation of natural resources. The need to generate export earnings to pay foreign debt is a problem faced by nearly all developing countries as well as the United States. Some, notably Brazil and Mexico, have debt burdens approaching or exceeding $100 billion. Merely to pay the interest on their loans, these countries have established fiscal and land-tenure policies designed to encourage production of export goods, such as beef and timber. In Brazil, cattle ranching has been supported with tax breaks and land acquisition rules that give title to individuals who "improve" the land. Improvements are generally defined as clearing the forest.

Elsewhere, to raise export revenues timber companies have been allowed to harvest timber at levels much greater than the

STRATEGIES THAT SAVE

Debt-for-Nature Swaps

Developing countries owe $1.3 trillion in foreign debt. This staggering amount is an important cause of tropical deforestation, as rainforest countries rapidly sell off their timber and convert rainforest to cattle pasture in order to raise money to pay off their loans. Recently, a new idea has allowed several countries to reduce their debt in exchange for committing resources to protect the rainforest. It is called debt-for-nature swap.

Groups like Conservation International and The Nature Conservancy purchase debt owed by rainforest countries to other nations or to banks. They are able to buy the debt in secondary markets at heavily discounted prices, reflecting the risk that a developing country may never pay the debt. For example, Conservation International bought $650,000 of Bolivia's debt for $100,000. Then, in exchange for a promise from the debtor country to set aside rainforest as natural reserve, the group holding the debt agrees to forgive the obligation. In the case of the Conservation International deal, Bolivia agreed to protect almost 6,000 square miles of rainforest. Costa Rica has agreed to set aside 355,000 acres in exchange for its debt reduction.

A few drawbacks that have yet to be ironed out have restricted the use of debt-for-nature swaps. These include their inflationary impact on the economies of developing countries, the erosion of political sovereignty, and their dubious enforceability. Some tropical countries object to having conditions placed on their own natural resources by other countries.

Despite their limited use, debt-for-nature swaps represent a good start in the fight to save rainforests throughout the world.

forest can sustainably support. These problems will not be alleviated until the debt burdens of these countries are substantially lowered.

Land tenure

The majority of good cropland in many tropical countries is owned by a very small and relatively well-off portion of the population. Because of the inequitable distribution of land, particularly in farm-based economies, there is an enormous gap between rich and poor. The small size of most of the farms is below the threshold of economic viability. This means that landless peasants are forced to clear more forest in order to scratch out a living.

In tropical Latin America, 7 percent of the population owns 90 percent of the arable land; the poorest third of the population owns 1 percent of the land. The percentages of rural households in Latin America that do not have enough land to support themselves are high: Brazil, 70 percent; Colombia, 66 percent; El Salvador, 60 percent; Guatemala, 85 percent; and Paraguay, 42 percent. The problem is not limited to Latin America. In Kenya, for example, the largest 3,000 farms control more land than the poorest 750,000 farms; 50 percent of all farms collectively own less than 15 percent of the land.

Although the causes of rainforest destruction can seem overwhelming at times, the problems are not insurmountable. Our involvement can go a long way toward helping to convince policymakers to reform many of the practices of the past.

CHAPTER FOUR

Red, White, and Blue Rainforests

Red, White, and Blue Rainforests

How U.S. tropical forests are being destroyed

Deforestation is not limited to Third World countries. The United States has tropical forests of its own, and these, too, are under assault. U.S. tropical forests are found on four groups of islands: Hawai`i, Puerto Rico, the U.S. Virgin Islands, and American Samoa. Although each boasts a variety of unique and colorful native species, they also share something with all other tropical forests: extremely vulnerable to human disturbance, these national treasures have suffered staggering losses.

These island groups are vastly different from other tropical forests and, in fact, differ greatly from each other. In most cases, forest destruction occurred a long time ago, as land was cleared for agricultural purposes. Today, the biggest threats are land development—urbanization and intensive recreational development. In addition, proposed geothermal and hydropower development projects threaten U.S. rainforests.

There are still important areas worth preserving, and it is possible to restore some of the areas that have been trashed. If allowed, native forests often grow back. As a result, there are important opportunities for protecting and restoring native habitats.

Hawai`i: Eden of endemic species

Flocks of scarlet `apapane ride the wind across the pali, the steep, eroded mountainsides. `Ohi`a trees blaze with salmon-colored and yellow blossoms. A thick understory of tangled plants reflects every shade of green. Aloha! This is Hawai`i's (native spelling) tropical forest, a lush jungle wilderness brightened with flowers that bloom nowhere else and with bird songs that are heard only here.

Hawai`i is justly famed for its hospitable climate and people, but it is also special in another respect: no other place on Earth, not even the famed Galapagos Islands, has a higher percentage of endemic plant and animal species—those occurring naturally nowhere else in the world. Almost 100 percent of Hawai`i's invertebrate species and nearly 90 percent of its birds and flowering plants are endemic.

Unfortunately, trouble has come to paradise. Hawai`i's native species are in jeopardy of becoming extinct. Nearly 40 percent of the islands' known endemic bird species have passed into oblivion already, victims of habitat destruction by human development and introduced plants and animals. Of the 42 bird species that remain, 30 have been officially classified as threatened or endangered. Hawai`i's two native mammals—the monk seal and the bat—are also designated as endangered, and about 40 percent of the native plants are considered endangered or are officially listed as candidates for such designation.

Hawai`i's crisis of extinction stems in part from the uniqueness of the state's natural heritage. Hawai`i was born from undersea volcanoes. Originally there were no plants or creatures living on the islands at all. Over 2,500 miles separate Hawai`i from the nearest continent. No islands on Earth are more geographically isolated. Only a handful of colonizers successfully made the long journey.

Because of Hawai`i's volcanic origin, its terrain is rugged; each island has a multitude of climates. The tortuous terrain restricted the movement of colonizing species. That condition, combined with the variable microclimates, caused species that arrived on the islands to "radiate," or evolve in ways that adapted to a specialized ecosystem.

Amazing examples of evolution's work abound in Hawai`i. From a single finch-like ancestor, for example, no fewer than 47 species or subspecies of birds evolved, far surpassing the 12 types of Galapagos finches that led Darwin to develop his theory of the evolution of the species. So high is the level of radiation, in fact, that scientists describe Hawai`i as the jewel in the crown that makes adaptive radiation on the other tropical islands pale in comparison.

Nature's grand experiment in supreme isolation led to the creation of a rich but vulnerable ecosystem. Nevertheless, Hawai`i succeeded in maintaining its delicate ecological balance until about 1,600 years ago. Then people arrived with their accompanying biological baggage—the domestic animals and plants they brought from their previous homes. The ensuing destruction of native habitat, along with the introduction of nonnative animals, insects, and plants, triggered a decline in native species that continues to this day.

The result of human encroachment has turned Hawai`i into the endangered-species capital of the United States. Fifty-five Hawaiian species and subspecies have been officially listed by the U.S. Fish and Wildlife Service as endangered or threatened. That amounts to about 10 percent of the total number for the entire country. No other state has more. Enough information is already available to support the addition of another 185 species to the official endangered list. The Hawaiian species on this list represent over a third of the total likely candidates in the United States.

Bats galore

There are nearly 1,000 kinds of bats worldwide. In tropical rainforests, bats can constitute more than half of all mammal species, and in some areas their biomass may equal more than half of all other mammals combined.

In the rainforests, bats are the most important seed-dispersing animals. They are also the primary pollinators of hundreds of tropical plants and trees. Bats contribute up to 95 percent of the seed dispersal that leads to forest regeneration. For more information, write to: Bat Conservation International, P.O. Box 162603, Austin, TX 78716.

There are several reasons for the high number of endangered species in Hawai`i. First is habitat conversion by man. Virtually all Hawaiian native plant communities have already been eliminated in lower elevations. Only about one-quarter of all Hawai`i remains as relatively intact natural habitat. The second factor, and currently the most pressing, is the introduction by man of nonnative plants and animals. Rats and mongooses prey on endemic birds, while pigs uproot trees in the rainforests and sheep and goats destroy the vegetation in drier habitats. Introduced plants invade and smother native vegetation. Foreign grasses also invade such areas, creating increased fire hazards and competing with native seedlings for space.

Why should we care whether Hawai`i's native species are

protected? To begin with, Hawai`i is a magnificent place with unique magic and beauty. To let it be destroyed, either by development or through carelessness, would be a tragedy. And from a scientific perspective, the answer is obvious. The phenomenal radiation patterns of Hawai`i's native species make it the best evolution lab in the world. Its wide range of soil and climate types provides scientists with a unique opportunity to study ecosystem function.

Native species are important for physical, aesthetic, and cultural reasons as well. Hawai`i's rainforests and cloud forests protect the integrity of its watersheds. And the Hawaiian culture has traditionally valued the land in its natural state for religious reasons.

Hawai`i's extinction crisis began long before the passage of federal and state laws designed to protect endangered species. Although current efforts are helpful, they remain insufficient, and the slide of many of Hawai`i's native species toward the brink of extinction continues unabated.

The principal federal law designed to protect native species and habitats is the Endangered Species Act. But because of personnel and budget limitations within the Fish and Wildlife Service, a large number of Hawaiian species that are indisputably imperiled have not been officially listed and consequently receive no formal protection under the Act.

Only 55 species out of a total of 333 thought to be imperiled have been officially listed as endangered or threatened. The pace of listing has been very slow in recent years, averaging only two or three Hawaiian species a year. No Hawaiian species were listed in 1987, 1988, or 1989.

Vigorous action on both the federal and state level will make the difference between paradise lost and paradise regained. Protection of Hawai`i's native species must be given a higher priority. We must encourage Congress and the state of Hawai`i to increase funding and staffing for endangered-species protection and recovery plans.

DEVELOPMENT THREAT

Protecting the Goddess of Fire

The Wao Kele O Puna rainforest, in the Puna district of the Big Island of Hawai`i, is one of the last lowland tropical forests in the United States. The forest is home to such rare native birds as the `apapane, the `omao, and the `amakihi, and to native trees like the `ohi`a. It is also a sacred religious site to native Hawaiian people.

A protected reserve until 1985, the Wao Kele O Puna is currently slated for a geothermal development that will bring about certain devastation of the forest. A project of the True Geothermal Company of Casper, Wyoming, the development would involve drilling six wells in as many as 35 sites of two to three acres apiece. Five power plants would be built on plots of five to eight acres each. The project would require up to 50 miles of roads, pipelines, and transmission corridors.

This network would provide expressways for nonnative plant and animal species to migrate into the region. The intrusion of such foreign species is considered a great threat.

Hawai`i's record of geothermal development does not inspire confidence; the state's first geothermal plant, a three-megawatt demonstration plant built for the Hawaiian Light and Power Company in 1981, has leaked highly toxic hydrogen sulfide gas, forcing evacuations. The proposed plant will be over 150 times as large as the demonstration facility. A local group of native Hawaiians opposes the project, saying drilling would violate their goddess Pele, who is said to reside in the steaming caldera.

Hawai`i lags far behind other states in promoting energy conservation, a much more reliable and economic energy source than geothermal development.

Preservation by ecosystem is the most effective way to protect many species simultaneously. Money is needed both to improve existing refuges and to acquire unprotected habitat.

Hakalau National Wildlife Refuge serves as a good example of how important these areas are. Located on the slopes of Mauna Kea, this exquisite remnant of Hawai`i's disappearing montane wet and mesic forests protects the habitat of five endangered bird species, the Hawaiian bat, and a variety of endemic plants. Yet without significant increases in funds for fencing, feral animal elimination, alien plant control, and native forest restoration, the refuge will rapidly lose its value as native species habitat, and the millions spent to acquire the land will have been wasted.

Hawai`i's four national parks also provide excellent opportunities to save what is left of the state's biological diversity. Because their level of endemism is high—the four parks include examples of 76 native natural communities, 42 percent of all those found in Hawai`i—and because their endemic populations are also severely threatened, the parks must be the highest priority in any National Park Service program to conserve biological diversity.

Haleakala National Park, for example, is a botanical marvel. The native koa and `ohi`a forests contain tree ferns and rare, spectacularly beautiful, endemic lobelioids and mints. It provides habitat for several endangered honeycreepers, some of them thought to be extinct until rediscovered here. It, too, needs more funds if it is to become a real refuge for endangered species.

We must also work to ensure that unfettered development is halted. One such project that threatens to destroy more of the Hawaiian rainforest is a proposed 500-megawatt geothermal project to be built in the Wao Kele O Puna rainforest on the Big Island of Hawai`i. The forest was a protected reserve until 1985. Construction of the drilling sites alone would require clear-cutting of some areas. Of even greater concern, the extensive network of roads required for exploration and development would further imperil the surviving populations of endemic species by allowing alien plants and animals easier access. Opponents of the project point out that the energy produced would be exported to the neighboring island of Oahu.

Other proposed projects for the island chain include numerous hydropower projects, a missile launching facility, condominium and resort developments, and a smelting plant for deep-sea mining of manganese and other minerals from the ocean bottom.

Puerto Rico: extinction in the enchanted isle

Picture the West Indies as a giant strand of pearl and jade cast upon the water. The center of this jewel-like Caribbean island chain is Puerto Rico, a 3,435-square-mile tropical U.S. commonwealth.

When Columbus landed in Puerto Rico in 1493, he found an island thick with forest and filled with wildlife. Nearly 500 years later, little of that original forest remains. Most has been cleared for agriculture, housing, and other development. Still, the remnants of natural Puerto Rico retain a bounty of biological riches. There are over 3,000 species of plants, 232 native bird species, 13 types of bats, and 78 species of reptiles and amphibians. The reptiles and amphibians have the highest level of endemism; three-quarters are found nowhere else.

Sadly, many of these species have been reduced to precariously small populations. To date, 35 wildlife and plant species have been listed by the Fish and Wildlife Service as endangered or threatened. Twenty-two of these are endemic to Puerto Rico. Among them are one-third of the endemic birds and nearly one-fifth of the endemic reptiles. Another dozen species have been listed by the commonwealth's Department of Natural Resources. Over 300 more species, primarily plants, are under consideration for federal listing.

Despite the past widespread habitat destruction, we now have important opportunities to save Puerto Rico's remaining natural heritage. Over the last 50 years, agricultural land use has decreased and second-growth forests have returned. These new forests have added to the important pockets of natural areas that survived the earlier clearing. The most important of them are found in the 4 percent of the island's area contained in the Caribbean National Forest and the 14 commonwealth forests. Other protected areas make up Puerto Rico's system of natural reserves. These forests and reserves represent a wide variety of ecosystems, from cloud forests to coastal mangroves to dry forests.

The loss of habitat in Puerto Rico has placed hundreds of native species in danger of extinction. Most of the remaining virgin forest is contained in the Caribbean National Forest, called "El Yunque." Like all national forests, it is managed by the U.S. Forest Service. An additional 14 forests—which in total area are twice as large as El Yunque—are managed by the commonwealth of Puerto Rico.

These forests contain a wide variety of forest types—wet montane forests, dry coastal scrub, forests on porous limestone (karst) and serpentine rocks, and mangroves. Unfortunately, they have often been managed unwisely. A management plan prepared by the Forest Service for El Yunque was deemed so inadequate that it was widely protested by the public, and a coalition of environmental groups went to court to block its implementation. No management plans for the commonwealth forests have yet been prepared.

El Yunque was hit hard by Hurricane Hugo in September 1989. Though the forest evolved in the presence of hurricanes and can presumably recover from such disruptions, the storm had a devastating effect on at least one of the forest's dependent endangered species, the Puerto Rican parrot. The small parrot population, already vulnerable as a result of past habitat loss, was reduced dramatically by the hurricane. Censuses indicate the bird's population declined from 47 to 23. More recently the number of sighted birds has plunged to six. So dire is the situation that the Fish and Wildlife Service is spending up to $1.28 million in special emergency funds to protect the surviving parrot population.

Although the Fish and Wildlife Service has responded to this emergency, funding for day-to-day conservation efforts in Puerto Rico has been so insufficient that the government can't meet its responsibilities. The commonwealth's endangered species protection programs have also been badly hampered by both inadequate funding and failure to enforce the regulations.

The problem is most extreme in six major geographical regions. Guánica Commonwealth Forest, located on the southwestern coast, is the largest remaining example of a subtropical dry forest in Puerto Rico. It has been designated as a biosphere reserve under the United Nations' Man and the Biosphere Program. Nearly 700 plant species occur in the forest, of which 11 are endemic. Half of the 141 Puerto Rican land-bird species live here. Nine are endemic.

Guánica provides a refuge for numerous endangered species, including the Puerto Rican nightjar, yellow-shouldered blackbird, Puerto Rican crested toad, hawksbill and leatherback sea turtles, and West Indian manatee. But a proposed tourist complex threatens their survival. It would increase traffic, insecticide use, and beach activities. The owner has offered to sell the land to conservation organizations for $1.8 million, but to date no buyer has stepped forward.

Inland from Guánica are two other commonwealth forests, Maricao and Susúa. Maricao represents a wet forest, with an average annual rainfall of 100 inches. Susúa, located only three miles away, is a climatic transition zone between the wet environment of the north and the dry coastal plains of the south. Numerous bird and plant species occur in both forests. There are 845 species of vascular plants in Maricao alone. Susúa is not as floristically diverse as Maricao, but it still boasts 157 arboreal species. Twenty-one are endemic. Both forests are threatened by deforestation, which is causing erosion, landslides, accelerated runoff, and flash flooding.

In the Mona passage between Puerto Rico and the Dominican Republic are located three small, uninhabited islands, Mona, Monito, and Descheo. The tropical dry forests of these islands contain a number of rare and endangered species, including the Mona ground iguana, a subspecies of the yellow-shouldered blackbird, and Monito gecko. But introduced animals such as black rats, rhesus monkeys, cats, and goats threaten these native species.

The northern part of Puerto Rico consists primarily of lowlands punctuated by numerous conical limestone hills as high as 160 feet, called "mogotes." The mogotes offer one of the world's finest examples of tropical karst—irregular limestone with sinks, underground streams, and caverns. Mining has endangered the fragile karst ecosystem. There are also heavy agricultural development, urbanization, road construction, and industrial pollution. A number of endangered species are at risk, including the Puerto Rican boa, Puerto Rican broad-winged hawk, beautiful goetzea, Vahl's boxwood, and St. Thomas prickly ash.

Construction of communication facilities atop the highest peaks in the Central Cordillera has disturbed the cloud forest ecosystem. Today at least two endemic plant species, the elfin tree fern and Cook's holly, have been pushed to the brink of extinction due to land disturbance and aggressive "weed" cutting to make room for antennas installed on peaks in Toro Negro Commonwealth Forest.

In addition, the principle wild population of the Puerto Rican plain pigeon is threatened by habitat destruction and shooting. The golden coqui, a frog that lives on bromeliads, is endemic to mountaintops on Cerro Avispa, Monte El Gato, and Sierra de Cayey. It, too, is threatened by habitat destruction and limited distribution. Another resident species of the Central

Cordillera, the Puerto Rican parrot, is also at risk. The eastern offshore waters of Puerto Rico provide important habitat for the endangered West Indian manatee. But coastal development, including dredging and marina construction, is degrading the area.

As in Hawai'i and the rest of the United States, Puerto Rico's endangered species are protected under the federal Endangered Species Act. Because of insufficient funding, however, listing and recovery efforts have fallen far short of what is needed. We must urge Congress to provide additional funding for endangered species protection in Puerto Rico and at the same time encourage the commonwealth government to step up its own protection efforts.

Opportunities to pursue environmental education in Puerto Rico also exist, especially after Hurricane Hugo. We should encourage the commonwealth to establish nature centers at representative regions of the island within its forest system in order to draw attention to the importance of the island's native tropical forests. These centers could include interpretive facilities; environmental education programs; and facilities for tropical forest management training, endangered species recovery, and recreation, research, and planning.

The U.S. Virgin Islands: behind the picture-postcard beauty

The Virgin Islands are like a picture postcard come to life. A verdant landscape gives way to white sand beaches bathed by aquamarine waters and warmed by a tropical sun. No wonder these three small Caribbean islands have been a coveted destination for winter-weary Americans for decades.

Their popularity, however, has not come without a price. The islands were largely deforested in past centuries when plantations grew sugar, cotton, and other crops and raised cattle. Some of the forests grew back in the twentieth century,

CLOSER TO HOME

NRDC and Tropical Forests in the United States

The Natural Resources Defense Council (NRDC) is a national nonprofit group made up of lawyers and scientists working to defend the environment. The organization works on several fronts to protect tropical rainforests in the United States and its territories. Activities include:

➤ Pressing for major increases in federal funding for the management and purchase of protected public lands in the U.S. tropics. NRDC's goal is to triple the federal commitment to these areas to a total of about $20 million.

➤ Working with the Fish and Wildlife Service, the federal agency charged with listing endangered species, to speed up the listing process and to provide better protection to listed species.

➤ Helping develop an alternative energy strategy for Hawai`i, one that would encourage the use of renewable energy sources and conservation and avoid further geothermal and hydropower development that destroys or damages Hawaiian rainforest.

➤ Monitoring the U.S. Forest Service's plans for the Caribbean National Forest (El Yunque) in Puerto Rico and working with the commonwealth to prepare management plans for its 14 forests.

but now the construction of homes and resort developments threatens both forested hills and coastal areas.

Even Virgin Islands National Park on St. John is in jeopardy. One-third of the area inside its boundaries is privately owned; some of the land is currently being developed. Siltation and other effects associated with development are constant threats. The park urgently requires economic assistance to offset the damage. Additional funds are needed for marker and mooring buoys to prevent the anchors of thousands of tour boats from damaging coral reefs and the sea-grass beds on which sea turtles depend for food. Efforts to control the introduced mongoose, which eats the eggs of native iguanas, sea turtles, and birds, must also be increased.

The Virgin Islands should create a territorial park system for numerous native habitats of wet and dry tropical forests and other biologically, scenically, and recreationally important lands.

Deforestation is a problem on privately owned forests on St. Thomas and St. Croix as well. Solutions are possible. For instance, conservationists are contemplating a combination of legal measures and private purchase agreements to protect natural resources. If habitat can be preserved, native plant species can be restored and wildlife protected.

American Samoa: lost horizons

The most pristine U.S. tropical forests grow on three tiny dots of land anchored near the dead center of the mighty Pacific Ocean. Just 76 square miles, American Samoa supports five distinct types of rainforest that stretch from sea to mountaintop: coastal, lowland, montane, ridge, and cloud.

Two species of fruit bats are partially responsible for the dense coverage of trees. The bats are voracious eaters and consequently help spread a lot of seeds, which in turn stimulates regeneration.

The principal reason for the largely intact forests is their isolation. In hopes of preventing resort development from becoming a threat, in 1988 Congress created a new national park in Samoa which protects forest and reef areas on the islands of Tutuila and Ta'u.

On Tutuila, the park contains extensive areas of undisturbed montane, lowland, and coastal tropical forests; montane scrub communities that include several endemic plant species; and an unusual ridge forest. The area boasts spectacular scenic views and hiking trails. The unique wildlife ranges from fairy terns and flightless rails to curious but gentle flying foxes. Samoan flying foxes have four-foot wingspans. They are unique among bats in being most active by day and in soaring on thermals like large birds. The area also protects several of Polynesia's most important archeological sites, including an ancient fortified village above Pago Pago Harbor and a large, relatively undisturbed prehistoric village. Both are greatly valued as part of Samoa's cultural heritage. The park's nine miles of scenic shoreline are also largely undisturbed.

On Ta'u, parklands protect an extensive cloud forest, one of only two such forests in American Samoa. The area contains many species of wildlife, including the only American occurrence of the Pacific boa. Thirty-five bird species have been identified within the park area, including the white-tailed tropicbird. The area is dominated by three indigenous tree species. There are also seven miles of pristine shoreline.

Proper management and additional conservation efforts in both designated areas will help ensure the continued survival of the rainforests of American Samoa.

We must act quickly if we are to protect these natural treasures and stop the loss of biological diversity. Preservation of the rainforests in Hawai`i, Puerto Rico, the U.S. Virgin Islands, and American Samoa can serve as a role model for other nations to follow. The United States is currently engaged in a number of efforts to convince other countries to protect their tropical forests. By protecting our own diverse native ecosystems, we will demonstrate that we, too, have the commitment required to protect the world's tropical forests.

CHAPTER FIVE

To See the Forest for the Trees

To See the Forest for the Trees

What you can do to help save the world's rainforests

The world's tropical rainforests can be saved. The myriad plant and animal species and indigenous tribes that depend on them for survival can be protected. And the greenhouse effect can be slowed. True, it won't be easy. The complex forces driving rainforest destruction can't be reversed overnight. But already headway is being made. Around the world people are taking actions to save the rainforests. Here in the United States, for example, public concern has increased awareness of the problem among political leaders. As a result, some of the policies stoking the crisis have been reformed. In the tropics, meanwhile, several countries have taken the first steps toward preserving their forests and the natural resources contained within them.

However, much, much more needs to be done. This is where you come in. Each of us can help save the world's tropical rainforests. There are many things individuals can do. But we must act quickly and decisively if we are to have any effect. Spreading the word about the need for rainforest protection, writing letters to the government, changing our purchasing habits, and supporting organizations that work to protect rainforests all help. Every effort will make a difference. Action is needed at all levels, and no effort is too small. So pick the rainforest protection activity that most appeals to you and go to it. A ☆ before an item indicates an activity to save U.S. rainforests.

Be an environmental consumer

➤ **Encourage local merchants to find out where their products come from.** Speak to merchants and ask them where their products come from. Tell them you don't want to buy rainforest products unless you can be sure they were grown or raised in a sustainable manner. Pay special attention to such merchandise as tropical wildlife (for instance, parrots, macaws, snakes, and lizards), tropical plants (orchids and bromeliads), curios, artifacts, and furniture made from tropical woods.

➤ **Avoid buying tropical lumber products unless you can be sure they are not endangered species and have been logged using sustainable methods.** The following tropical hardwoods all come from rainforests:

Apitong
Banak
Bocote
Bubinga
Cocobolo
Cordia
Ebony
Goncalo avles
Greenheart
Iroko
Jelutang
Koa
Lauan
Mahogany
Meranti
Padauk
Purpleheart
Ramin
Rosewood
Satinwood
Teak
Virola
Wenge
Zebrawood

➤ **Avoid purchasing beef produced in countries where you know that tropical forests are being systematically cleared for pasture.** Since little information exists about the origin of

RAINFOREST PRODUCTS

Shopping for the Rainforests

Cupuacu yogurt? Babacu oil? Copaiba shampoo? Patchouli-root soap? Priprioca perfume? Sound unfamiliar? To most U.S. consumers, they undoubtedly are, but they may not be for long. These and other rainforest products may soon be coming to a store near you. It's all part of helping to save rainforests.

Products such as these promise to make the rainforest economically productive without threatening its survival. The key is that they can be sustainably extracted.

Nearly one of six rainforest species can yield some direct economic use other than timber. Rattans, latex, resins, fruits, nuts, and medicinal plants offer alternative economic values to rainforest logging. Dubbed "minor forest products" by governments and international development agencies, these nontimber uses of the rainforest have traditionally been ignored in development planning decisions.

To develop markets for rainforest items that can be removed in a sustainable manner, groups like Cultural Survival, of Boston, Massachusetts, and Community Products, Inc., of Montpelier, Vermont, are introducing fruits, nuts, and oils to American and European consumers. The Body Shop, a British organic cosmetics company, sells hair conditioner based on Brazil nut oil. Ralston Purina Company is testing rainforest ingredients for use in breakfast cereals.

By demonstrating to rainforest governments the value of intact rainforests in very real terms, namely export earnings, these groups are saving the rainforest from the chain saw and fire. In response, Brazil has established extractive reserves totaling over 8,000 square miles.

rainforest beef, ask Congress to pass a beef labeling law that specifies the country of origin. For more information, contact the Rainforest Action Network. It publishes a newsletter that contains up-to-date news on this issue. The address is in Chapter 6.

➤ **Support products that sustain the rainforest.** Certain companies are going out of their way to develop products that help support the rainforest. Ben & Jerry's Homemade Ice Cream, for example, sells a Rain Forest Buttercrunch candy and ice cream that uses Brazil nuts bought from Amazon harvesters. The Body Shop, an environmentally concerned cosmetics chain based in England that has stores throughout the United States, is developing a line of skin-care products made from rainforest plants. See box on page 90 for more information.

➤ **Visit the rainforest.** By visiting rainforests, you will help make them an economic asset. "Ecotourism" is quickly becoming an important factor in saving rainforests. Rainforest national parks attract foreign tourists, provide income for cities and towns throughout the region, and supply jobs for locals, who are trained as rangers, researchers, and guides.

If you have visited a tropical country, or plan to, write to that country's officials to tell them that as a tourist you are interested in the preservation of their tropical forests. See box on page 93 for more information.

☆ **Visit U.S. rainforests.** Spend your vacation touring the rainforests of Hawai`i, Puerto Rico, the Virgin Islands, and American Samoa. Write to their chambers of commerce and visitor bureaus and tell them how important these natural attractions are.

☆ **Plant a tree in the Hawaiian rainforest.** Become a member of NRDC, for $10 or more, and they will plant a Koa tree in your name in an endangered rainforest on the island of Hawai`i. For more information, see page 112.

➤ **Adopt an acre of rainforest.** The Nature Conservancy has launched an Adopt-an-Acre Program in which you can buy protection of specific acres of threatened rainforest. For $30 you will receive an honorary land deed. All funds support the acquisition of rainforest land. For more information, write Adopt-an-Acre Program, The Nature Conservancy, 1815 N. Lynn St., Arlington, VA 22209.

For $25, you can become a Guardian of the Amazon through the World Wildlife Fund. The money is used to set aside land; hire local people to fence it in, put up signs, and protect it; teach locals how to successfully harvest rainforest crops and products; and help tribes protect their land from devastation. For more information, contact World Wildlife Fund/Canada at 416-923-8173, or write: WWF, 60 St. Clair Ave. E., Suite 201, Toronto, Ontario M4T 1N5.

Home remedies

➤ **Increase paper recycling.** Recycling your newspapers at home as well as white paper at the office will reduce the demand for both tropical and temperate timber. Such conservation can help halt the harvest of old-growth forests here at home.

➤ **Be more energy efficient.** Weatherizing your home and using energy-efficient appliances and lighting will show the world that individual investments in energy efficiency can reduce the need to construct more dams and power plants for generating electricity. Dam construction in the rainforest accelerates deforestation.

Keep your car tuned up for better fuel efficiency. Carpool or use public transit whenever possible. Burning fossil fuels such as gasoline contributes to global warming, a situation exacerbated by deforestation. There are many things you can do to conserve energy and make your home more energy efficient. For additional information, send $3.95 to: Energy Book, The Earthworks Group, 1400 Shattuck Ave., #25, Berkeley, CA 94709,

ECOTOURISM

New Trends in Travel

Tourism presents another attractive and sustainable alternative to rainforest logging. "Ecotourism" is a growth industry: the number of foreign tourists arriving in Manaus, Brazil, the heart of the Amazon rainforest, increased to over 70,000 in 1988 from 12,000 in 1983. In an effort to draw tourists, Costa Rica now advertises the wonders of its rainforests and other natural resources in U.S. magazines.

It stands to reason that if countries realize the economic benefits of preserving their rainforests in order to attract tourist dollars, they will do much to protect them.

As we have seen in this country, tourism—if improperly managed—can also destroy forests. Tourists should consult the environmental organizations listed in Chapter 6 when choosing countries to visit and tour operators to patronize. Make sure that both park managers and tour operators are ecologically responsible.

A number of groups organize expeditions to the rainforest. They include:

Conservation International, 1015 18th St., NW, Suite 1002, Washington, DC 20036.

Earthwatch, 680 Mt. Auburn St., Box 403, Watertown, MA 02272, 617-926-8200.

International Expeditions, 1776 Independence Court , Birmingham, AL 35216, 800-633-4734.

New York Botanical Garden, Travel Program Coordinator, Bronx, NY 10458, 212-220-8700.

Sobek Expeditions, P.O. Box 1089, Suite 1002, Angels Camp, CA 95222, 800-777-7939.

Victor Emanuel Nature Tours, Box 33008, Austin, TX 78764, 800-328-8368.

for a copy of its *30 Simple Energy Things You Can Do to Save the Earth*.

➤ **Build a backyard wildlife refuge.** Many of North America's most popular songbirds are actually migrants from the rainforests of Central and South America. By putting up birdfeeders and planting appropriate vegetation, you can provide them with a welcome stopover on their long flights. The National Wildlife Federation has a program that can help you build an effective refuge. For information, write to: NWF Backyard Wildlife Habitat Program, 1400 16th St., NW, Washington, DC 20036-2266.

Spread the word

➤ **Share your knowledge of the importance of tropical forests with others.** Helping to increase awareness among others about the plight of the world's rainforests is probably the single most important thing you can do. When enough people learn about the problem, our collective power will produce change. There are many ways to do this.

• Tell your friends, neighbors, and coworkers about the rainforest.

• Schedule programs, workshops, and meetings on tropical forest conservation at your school, church, club, or office.

• Buy a copy of this book for your local library.

• Enlist the help of universities and colleges in your area in presenting community programs, talking to the media, and learning about further sources of information.

• Encourage local school teachers to include information about tropical forests in their classes. Hold a workshop for teachers, and supply them with information to help them get in touch with people who are knowledgeable about tropical forests issues. There is a listing of Teacher Guides in Chapter 6.

• Sponsor programs with rainforest themes, such as a writing or poster contest, film festival, run, cooking contest, musical or storytelling program, travelogue, public debate, letter-writing campaign, cleanup day for a local natural area, presentation for schoolchildren, partnership with a sister city in the tropics, or an education campaign about tropical forest products used or manufactured in your area.

• Encourage organizations to buy this book in bulk and distribute it to their members and others. Proceeds from bulk orders help preserve rainforests and other threatened environments. For more information on ordering, see page 112.

➤ **Enlist media support.** Write a letter expressing your opinion to the editor of your local newspaper. Letters to the editor are printed in the editorial section. Such a letter will not only inform other citizens about the rainforest crisis, but it will also let the editor know that this issue is important to the paper's readers. This will help gain more space for future rainforest-related news articles. The media is invaluable in the effort to focus public opinion and motivate elected officials and policymakers to act on behalf of rainforest protection.

Join a rainforest protection group

Look for other people and organizations in your community that may already be involved in saving tropical forests, and join in their work. Many conservation-minded groups are actively working to protect the world's tropical rainforests. They need your support. The old adage about strength in numbers has never rung more true. These groups can provide you with the means to get more involved in the rainforest preservation struggle. They are also an excellent information resource. Their addresses are in Chapter 6.

➤ **Volunteer your time.** Everyone has something that he or she does well, and every organization needs help.

➤ **Donate money.** Even a small donation will be welcomed. Request the annual report of a conservation group that interests you, then earmark your contribution for a specific project that looks promising. Most are tax deductible. Find out if your company matches donations made by employees. Support local conservation groups in tropical countries that work to save their tropical forests. Often their success depends upon economic and moral support from outside their own borders. You will find a list of organizations in Chapter 6.

➤ **If there isn't an organization operating in your community, start one.**

Teach your children

➤ **To help increase your children's awareness, read them books about the rainforests or give them books they can read themselves.** You can find plenty of books at your local library. A list of children's books is contained in Chapter 6. Play your children an audiotape to introduce them to the sounds of the rainforest. A wonderful tape called "Amazon Days, Amazon Nights" is available from NRDC for $7.95. It comes with notes that identify all the rainforest animals on the tape. To order, see page 112.

➤ **Help your children organize a letter-writing campaign.** Encourage your children to draw a picture of the rainforest or write a letter and send it to elected officials and corporations. These can have real impact.

➤ **Help teachers develop a rainforest curriculum for school.** The World Wildlife Fund has produced a special environmental education package, *The Vanishing Rain Forests.* This education kit, designed for grades 2 through 6, consists of a 28-page booklet, teacher's manual, posters, and six-minute video. You may purchase the kit for $29.95. To order yours, contact WWF, P.O. Box 4866, Hampden Post Office, Baltimore, MD 21211; 301-338-6951. The Rainforest Action Network also publishes a teacher's guide. Contact them for one.

➤ **Organize a "Rainforest Awareness Week" at your children's school.** You can get an information packet created by high school students, *How to Organize a Rainforest Awareness Week at Your School*, from Creating Our Future, 398 North Ferndale, Mill Valley, CA 94941; 415-381-6744.

➤ **Help your children take up a collection to donate to conservation groups.** Holding walkathons, bake sales, and rummage sales are just a few of the creative ways kids can raise money.

➤ **Encourage your children to "plant a rainforest tree" or "adopt an acre" of rainforest.** See pages 91 and 92 for details.

➤ **Help your children's school adopt a sister school in a tropical country.** The ensuing exchange of ideas can both help your own child understand the problems of the rainforest and educate the children in the other countries, not to mention lending them moral support. After all, these children will be the leaders of the next generation.

Address the problem

➤ **Write your elected officials.** In the battle to save the world's rainforests, the pen *is* mightier than the sword. Writing letters to policymakers is one of the most effective tools for change there is. Every letter counts. Write to your elected officials, your senators, congressional representatives, governor, state legislators, mayor, and city council members. Tell them why you are concerned about rainforest destruction, and ask them what they are doing to help prevent it. In addition, ask your friends, neighbors, and relatives to write letters.

You can also call your elected officials. If you can't speak with them directly, talk with one of their aides. Ask for the staffer who works on environmental and international issues.

Explain your concerns and ask what his or her boss is doing about protecting the rainforest. Remember, staffers are the ones who advise elected officials on key issues and keep them informed about their constituents' opinions.

You can find out how to contact your elected representatives by calling your local voter registration office, which is listed in the government section of the phone book.

Also, write to the president of the United States and the members of his cabinet, especially the secretaries of state, agriculture, and treasury. They have tremendous influence on tropical rainforest policy. Their addresses are:

President George Bush, The White House,1600 Pennsylvania Ave., NW, Washington, DC 20500.

James Baker, Secretary of State, U.S. State Department, 2201 C St., NW, Washington, DC 20520.

Nicholas Brady, Secretary of Treasury, U.S. Treasury Department, 1500 Pennsylvania Ave., NW, Washington, DC 20250.

Clayton Yeutter, Secretary of Agriculture, U.S. Department of Agriculture, 14th St. & Independence, SW, Washington, DC 20250.

☆ **Ask Congress to fund protection of our own U.S. rainforests.** Funds are needed to protect the rainforests in Hawai`i, Puerto Rico, the Virgin Islands, and American Samoa. Congress needs to increase appropriations for these areas in order to acquire and maintain critical habitat. Write to NRDC and request a more detailed report of recommendations for protecting each of these American tropical forests.

☆ **Write to Hawai`i's governor and ask him to increase protective measures for the state's rainforests.** Specifically, ask the governor to halt all construction of roads in biologically critical areas; defer geothermal exploration and development; inventory all state-owned native ecosystems that have been leased; develop and implement a protection strategy for priority native ecosystems; design and implement effective alien-species control programs; and establish a natural area reserves fund. His address is: Governor John D. Waihee III, Executive Chamber, State Capitol, Honolulu, HI 96813.

☆ **Write to the Pele Defense Fund** to learn more about how native Hawaiians are struggling to protect rainforests from destruction by geothermal plants. Their address is in Chapter 6.

➤ **Participate in World Bank decisions.** The World Bank and other agencies have a history of funding and supporting rainforest-killing development projects. This needs to change. Communicate your views on saving tropical forests to the agencies and development banks that provide loans to tropical countries. Urge them to stop financing rainforest dams and highways and to fund instead small-scale projects that benefit rainforests and their inhabitants. The World Bank is beginning to perform reviews of the environmental consequences of some of their lending projects. These reviews are called Environmental Impact Assessments (EIAs). Write to the World Bank and request the EIAs. Read them and send your comments back so your voice will be heard in the decision-making process. Write to:

President, The World Bank, 1818 H St., NW, Washington, DC 20433.

Administrator, U.S. Agency for International Development, 320 21st St., NW, Washington, DC 20577.

President, Inter-American Development Bank, 1808 17th St., NW, Washington, DC 20577.

➤ **Support development of international laws.** Deforestation of the world's tropical rainforests is an international problem. Ask the secretary-general of the United Nations to hold a special session of the UN on tropical rainforest protection. Encourage the development of international standards for good forestry practices. Write to: Secretary-General, United Nations, New York, NY 10017.

➤ **Encourage tropical countries to enact their own laws to protect their rainforests.** The age of the global village is upon us. Mass media and satellite communication have seen to that. Never before has world opinion been such a powerful tool. To those leaders who are working diligently to protect their country's rainforests, send letters of support. Conversely, your letters can condemn those who are not. The Rainforest Action Network regularly publishes action alerts that can tell you which countries are doing what. Foreign organizations can also supply you with information. You'll find addresses in Chapter 6.

➤ **Write to corporations.** Many corporations trade in rainforest products. Some of them engage in business practices that promote rainforest destruction, rather than the sustainable management of natural resources. Write to them and ask what they are doing to protect the rainforests. Tell them you wish to avoid buying products that don't make wise use of the rainforests. A list of addresses is contained in Chapter 6.

☆ **Write to the True Geothermal Co. and voice your support of protection for the Hawaiian rainforest.** The True Geothermal Co. proposes to build a huge geothermal development project on the Big Island of Hawai`i. Write to: H.A. True, Jr., President, True Geothermal Co., P.O. Box 2360, Casper, WY 82602.

Law of the jungle

☆ **Urge your elected officials to vote for laws that support rainforest protection.** Participation in the democratic process is an important means of influencing the role of the U.S. government in protecting tropical forests. New laws are needed to stop the destruction of the world's rainforests. When proposed, they need your support. To keep abreast, ask your elected officials to inform you of proposed rainforest bills.

☆ **Register to vote . . . and vote.** Voting is the most direct means of influencing the political process. Examine the environmental voting records of each candidate. Make environmental issues a primary criterion for choosing a candidate. To monitor voting records, contact: The League of Conservation Voters, 1150 Connecticut Avenue, NW, Suite 201, Washington, DC 20036.

☆ **Specifically, support:**

- the preservation of U.S. tropical and old-growth forests
- U.S. assistance for the United Nations Fund for Population Activities
- preferential trading status for tropical timber that is sustainably extracted
- efforts to provide international debt relief to tropical countries through the Brady Plan
- a ban on exporting deadly pesticides to tropical countries
- a beef labeling law that specifies the country of origin

The actions listed here will go a long way toward helping end the destruction of the rainforests, but only if each and every one of us gets involved. Taking these steps may seem like a lot for any one person to do, so just do what you can, even if it means writing just one letter. Remember, every little bit helps; there *is* strength in numbers. Consider this: if every citizen in the United States gave one nickel, we could raise the $12 million necessary to protect our Hawaiian tropical forests and the 300 most endangered species that live there.

If the rainforests of the world are to have any chance at all of surviving, it is up to us. We can make a difference, but we must act now. Tomorrow will be too late.

CHAPTER SIX

Natural Resources

Natural Resources

Where to get additional information

Many organizations are involved in the fight to save the world's rainforests. Not only are they excellent sources of additional information, but they can provide you with ways to become active participants in the struggle as well.

U.S. organizations involved in saving tropical rainforests

Conservation International, 1015 18th St., NW, Suite 1002, Washington, DC 20036.

Cultural Survival, 11 Divinity Ave., Cambridge, MA 02138.

Environmental Defense Fund, 1616 P St., NW, Suite 150, Washington, DC 20036.

Friends of the Earth/U.S., 218 D St., SE, Washington, DC 20003.

Global Tomorrow Coalition, 1325 G St., NW, Suite 915, Washington, DC 20005.

Greenpeace, 1436 U St., NW, Washington, DC 20009.

International Planned Parenthood Federation, 902 Broadway, 10th Floor, New York, NY 10010.

National Audubon Society, 645 Pennsylvania Ave., SE, Washington, DC 20003.

National Museum of Natural History/Smithsonian Institution, Washington, DC 20008.

National Wildlife Federation, 1400 16th St., NW, Washington, DC 20036.

National Zoological Park/Smithsonian Institution, Washington, DC 20008.

Natural Resources Defense Council, 40 W. 20th St., New York, NY 10011.

The Nature Conservancy, 1800 North Kent St., Arlington, VA 22209.

Pele Defense Fund, P.O. Box 404, Volcano, HI 96875.

Population Crisis Committee, 1120 19th St., NW, Suite 550, Washington, DC 20036.

Rainforest Action Network, 301 Broadway, Suite A, San Francisco, CA 94133.

Rainforest Alliance, 270 Lafayette St., Suite 512, New York, NY 10012.

The Rainforest Foundation, Inc., 1776 Broadway, 14th Floor, New York, NY 10019.

Sierra Club, 730 Polk St., San Francisco, CA 94109.

Smithsonian Tropical Research Institute, APO Miami, FL 34002.

Survival International USA, 2121 Decatur Place, NW, Washington, DC 20008.

World Resources Institute, 1735 New York Ave., NW, Washington, DC 20006.

World Wildlife Fund/Conservation Foundation, 1250 24th St., NW, Washington, DC 20037.

Zero Population Growth Inc., 1400 10th St., NW, Suite 320, Washington, DC 20036.

Foreign organizations involved in saving rainforests

Campa a Amazonia: Por la Vida, P.O. Box 246C, Quito, Ecuador.

COICA (Coordinating Body for the Indigenous Peoples' Organizations of the Amazon Basin), Jiron Almagro 614, Lima 11, Peru.

Environmental Foundation Ltd., 6 Boyd Place, Colombo 3, Sri Lanka.

Friends of the Earth/U.K., 2628 Underwood St., London N17JU, United Kingdom.

Haribon Foundation, Suite 306, Sunrise Condo, Ortegas Ave., San Juan, Metro Manilla, Philippines.

Indonesian Environmental Forum (WALHI), J1, Penjernihan I, Kompl. Kenangan 15, Pejompongan, Jakarta 10210, Indonesia.

International Union for the Conservation of Nature and Natural Resources, Avenue Mont Blanc, 1196 Gland, Switzerland.

Probe International, 225 Brunswick Ave., Toronto, Ontario M5S 2M6, Canada.

Research Institute for Natural Resource Policy, 105 Rajpur Rd., Dehra Dun, Uttar Pradesh 248001, India.

World Rainforest Movement, 87 Contonment Road, 10250 Penang, Malaysia.

World Wildlife Fund/U.K., Panda House, Godalming, Surrey, GU7 1XR, United Kingdom.

Corporations

According to *Tropical Hardwoods*, published by the Rainforest Action Network in 1989, the following is a list of addresses and the names of chief executive officers (CEOs) of some U.S. companies that have subsidiaries involved in tropical deforestation. Write, call, or do whatever you think is appropriate to urge these corporations to make sure they are trading in only sustainably managed rainforest products. This list is subject to change—write to Rainforest Action Network for list updates.

Boise Cascade Corp., One Jefferson Square, P.O. Box 50, Boise, ID 83728, 208-384-6161, John H. Miller, CEO.

Champion International, One Champion Plaza, Stamford, CT 06921, 203-358-7000, Andrew C. Sigler, CEO.

Georgia-Pacific Corp., 133 Peachtree St., NE, P.O. Box 105605, Atlanta, GA 30303, 404-521-4000, T. Marshall Hahn, Jr., CEO.

Great Northern Nekoosa, 401 Merritt 7, P.O. Box 5120, Norwalk, CT 06856, 203-845-9000, William R. Ladig, CEO.

International Paper, Two Manhattanville Rd., Purchase, NY 10577, 914-397-1500, John A. Georges, CEO.

Kimberly-Clark, Texas Commerce Tower, 545 E. John Carpenter Fwy, Irving, TX 75062, *or* P.O. Box 619100, DFW Airport Sta., Dallas, TX 75261, 214-830-1200, Darwin E. Smith, CEO.

Weyerhauser Company, Tacoma, WA 98477, 206-924-2345, George H. Weyerhauser, CEO.

As of this writing, the following companies are in varying stages of exploration and extraction of petroleum in the Oriente (the Ecuadorian Amazon). Do whatever you think appropriate to urge them to conduct their business in an environmentally sound manner. For an updated list, write to NRDC.

Arco International Oil and Gas, 515 S. Flower St., Los Angeles, CA 90071, 213-486-3511, John Middleton, CEO.

Conoco Inc., 600 N. Dairy Ashford Road, Houston, TX 77079, 713-293-1000, Constantine S. Nicandros, CEO.

Occidental Petroleum, 10889 Wilshire Boulevard, Los Angeles, CA 90024, 213-879-1700, Ray Irani, CEO.

Texaco, Inc., 2000 Westchester Ave., White Plains, NY 10650, 914-253-7056, James W. Kinnear, CEO.

Unocal, 1201 W. 5th St., Los Angeles, CA 90017, 213-977-7600, Richard Stegemeir, CEO.

Recommended reading

Amazon Resource and Action Guide, Rainforest Action Network, 1990.

Biodiversity, E.O. Wilson, National Academy Press, 1988.

The Decade of Destruction, Adrian Cowell, Henry Holt, 1990.

The Deluge and the Ark: A Journey into Primate Worlds, Dale Peterson, Houghton Mifflin Co., 1989.

Dreams of Amazonia, Roger Stone, Penguin Books, 1985.

The Enchanted Canopy, Andrew W. Mitchell, Macmillan, 1986.

In the Rainforest: Report from a Strange, Beautiful, Imperiled World, Catherine Caufield, University of Chicago Press, 1984.

Jungles, Edward S. Ayensu, Crown Publisher, Inc., 1980.

Lessons of the Rainforest, Suzanne Head and Robert Heinzman, Sierra Club Books, 1990.

Life Above the Jungle Floor, Donald Perry, Simon & Schuster, 1986.

People of the Tropical Rain Forest, edited by Julie Denslow and Christine Padoch, University of California Press, 1988.

The Primary Source, Norman Myers, W. W. Norton & Co., 1984.

Race to Save the Tropics, edited by Robert Goodland, Island Press, 1990.

Saving the Tropical Forests, Judith Gradwohl and Russell Greenberg, Island Press, 1988.

Tropical Forest Conservation, WWF International, 1989.

Tropical Hardwoods: A Report, Mike Roselle and Tracy Katelman, Rainforest Action Network, 1989.

Tropical Nature, Andrew Forsyth and Kenneth Miyata, Charles Scribner & Sons, 1984.

Tropical Rainforest, Arnold Newman, Facts on File, 1990.

The Tropical Rain Forest: A First Encounter, Marius Jacobs, Springer-Verlag, 1988.

Especially for children

Color the Rainforest, Living Planet Press, 1990. Available from NRDC for $4.95. To order, see page 112.

The Great Kapok Tree, Lynne Cherry, Gulliver Books/Harcourt Brace Jovanovich, 1990.

Headhunters and Hummingbirds: An Expedition into Ecuador, Robert Peck, Walker & Co., 1987.

Nature Hide & Seek: Jungles, John Norris Wood and Kevin Dean, Methuen Children's Books, 1987.

P3/The Earth-based Magazine for Kids (a monthly environmental magazine for ages 6 to 12). Subscription costs $14. Write to P.O. Box 52, Montgomery, VT 05470.

The Tropical Rain Forest, Jean Craighead George, Crowell, 1990.

Audiovisual materials

Amazonia: A Celebration of Life (1985). Andrew Young, Blinn Road, Croton-On-Hudson, NY 10520.

Banking on Disaster. Bullfrog Films, Oley, PA, 215-779-8226.

BioDiversity (1987). National Academy Press, 2101 Constitution Ave., NW, Washington, DC 20418. $24.50.

Death in the Rainforest (1988). BBC Enterprises, Woodlands, 80 Wood Lane, London W12 0TT, Telex 9344678.

Earth First! (1987). VHS. Educational Film and Video Project, 5332 College Ave., Suite 101, Oakland, CA 94618, 415-655-9050. Rental $35/one week. Sale $39.95 + $4.95 for shipping.

Equatorial River: The Amazon (1988). Bullfrog Films, Oley, PA 19547, 800-543-FROG. Video purchase $285. Film purchase $470. Rental $45.

Firsthand. Cultural Survival, 11 Divinity Ave., Cambridge, MA 02138. $12 each + $1 postage.

Mayan Rainforest Farming (1987). Bullfrog Films, Oley, PA 19547, 215-779-8226. Rental $50. Sale $195 ($210, 3/4").

Our Threatened Heritage (1987). National Wildlife Federation, International Programs, 1412 16th St., NW, Washington, DC 20036, 202-637-3776. Sale $20.

Rainforest Rap (1988). World Wildlife Fund, P.O. Box 4866, Hamdon Post Office, Baltimore, MD 21211, 516-444-3132. Sale $15.

The Vanishing Forest: The Crisis of Tropical Deforestation. Knowledge Unlimited, P.O. Box 52, Madison, WI 57301, 800-356-2303. $35.

Teacher guides

Review notes are courtesy of Creating Our Future (see page 97).

Environmental Education about the Rain Forest, by Klaus Berkmuller. A good working handbook. Scientific information along with sensitive examples that illustrate real-life ethical, aesthetic, cultural, scientific, ecological, and economic value choices. Published by IUCN/WWF. Available for $10 in English or Spanish from Wildland Management Center, School of Natural Resources, University of Michigan, Ann Arbor, MI 48109.

Our Threatened Heritage. Curriculum booklet for an 18-minute video (designed for use with high school students or in training workshops) about tropical rainforests, their ecology, and reasons they are threatened. $20.00 for booklet and video. National Wildlife Federation, International Programs, 1400 16th St., NW, Washington, DC 20036, 202-637-3776.

Rainforests: A Teacher's Resource Guide. This very thorough and up-to-date 28-page resource guide was compiled and designed by Lynne Chase of Southern Regional High School in Manahawkin, NJ. Available for $5 from the Rainforest Action Network, 301 Broadway, Suite A, San Francisco, CA 94133.

About the author

Scott Lewis was born in New York City and raised in Portland, Oregon, where he spent much of his youth among the temperate rainforests of the Pacific Northwest. After graduating from Colorado College and Stanford Law School, Scott traveled extensively in South America and Asia, and has worked as an analyst for energy and environmental policy in the national political arena. This is his first book.

About the Natural Resources Defense Council

NRDC is one of the nation's premier environmental protection organizations. Now celebrating its 20th anniversary, NRDC is backed by 140,000 members and has a staff of over 80 lawyers, scientists, and environmental specialists working in five offices nationwide. NRDC led the successful citizen fights against lead in gasoline, CFCs in aerosols, and Alar in apples. The organization has also worked for more than 15 years with environmentalists in Africa, Asia, and Latin America to protect tropical rainforests. NRDC has been a leader in reforming the policies and projects of the World Bank, the U.S. Agency for International Development, and other international development agencies. In 1990, NRDC is launching a major public education campaign to help save our nation's unique and vanishing tropical forests in Hawai`i, Puerto Rico, the U.S. Virgin Islands, and American Samoa.

NRDC Rainforest Rescue Products

All proceeds from these NRDC sales go to rainforest preservation and other programs in defense of threatened environments.

The Rainforest Book—How You Can Save the World's Rainforests

112 pages, $5.95; **Item #101**

Special discounts are available for bulk orders. Call 212-727-4486

Color the Rainforest

This spectacular coloring book is every child's introduction to the magic and wonder of the rainforest. Ages 3-7. 48 pages; $4.95; **Item #102**

Amazon Days, Amazon Nights—an audio adventure

Enter the mysterious world of the Amazon jungle through this beautiful hi-fidelity audiotape. Great for all ages. 40 minute cassette; $7.95; **Item #103**

Rescue the Rainforest T-Shirt

Wear the brilliant hues of the rainforest with this beautiful T-shirt, created from the cover art of *The Rainforest Book*. 100% premium cotton.

Adult size: $14.95; **Item #104** Child size: $12.95; **Item #105**

Cut out or copy form below, and mail with your check to:
NRDC, P.O. Box 1400, Church Hill, MD 21690

Ordering instructions

QTY	ITEM #	UNIT PRICE	TOTAL
	107	DONATION	$
		SHIPPING	$ 2.00
		TOTAL	$

• Please add $2.00 for shipping.

• Please make your check or money order payable to NRDC and send to: NRDC, P.O. Box 1400, Church Hill, MD 21690.

Name: ____________________

Address: ____________________

____

• **Call 1-800-327-1400** to become a member of NRDC for $10 or more. NRDC will plant a Koa tree in your name in an endangered Hawaiian rainforest. Give $30 or more and get a free Rescue the Rainforest T-shirt. Have a credit card ready (or use this order form to donate).